Forza! uno
Teacher's Manual

Michael Sedunary

CIS·Heinemann

CIS•Heinemann

A division of Reed International Books Australia Pty Ltd

22 Salmon Street, Port Melbourne, Victoria 3207

Telephone (03) 9245 7111

Facsimile (03) 9245 7333

World Wide Web http://www.reedbooks.com.au

Email heinemann@reedbooks.com.au

Offices in Sydney, Brisbane, Adelaide and Perth. Associated companies, branches and representatives around the world.

© CIS•Heinemann 1997

First published 1997

Author: Michael Sedunary

Illustrated by Con Aslanis

Edited by Jo Horsburgh

Editorial contributions: Hilary Royston

Designed by Robert Bertagni

Cover design by Robert Bertagni

Production by Cindy Smith

Printed and bound in Australia by Southbank Book

ISBN 1 86391 535 4.

Contents

How to use *Forza! uno*   v

Capitolo 1   Questa è la mia classe   1

Capitolo 2   Ti piace?   10

Capitolo 3   A casa con i Ferraro   20

Capitolo 4   Dal veterinario   33

Capitolo 5   Non c'è niente da fare!   45

Capitolo 6   In giro a Roma   55

Capitolo 7   Maura fa la spesa   68

Capitolo 8   Un uomo moderno   77

In the **Prefazione** to the *Textbook*, students are alerted to the fact that '*Forza!* is not the sort of book you just go through page by page.' They are told that they will have to get used to going backwards and forwards to the different sections of a chapter as well as combining material from the *Textbook*, *Workbook* and *Cassettes*.

This is where the *Teacher's Manual* comes in. The body of this book contains chapter-by-chapter suggestions for the sequencing and integration of the various elements of the course, so that your students get a good balance of practice for their listening, speaking, reading and writing skills.

How to use *Forza! uno* offers a separate consideration of each of these elements, with detailed, practical ideas on how to exploit them in the classroom. You may find it useful to return to it from time to time, to remind yourself of the different approaches you can take to each one.

Textbook

Fotoromanzi and fumetti

As well as establishing the theme for each chapter, the **fotoromanzi** (photo-stories) and **fumetti** (cartoon stories) are the primary fund of language, a storehouse of expressions generating a wealth of communicative activity. The idea of placing a story at the beginning of the chapter is to let students experience the language in action, to see it and hear it in a context that will stimulate their interest and motivate them to want to use it.

Since each story contains a substantial amount of new language, one of the main tasks in the classroom is to gradually whittle away problems of comprehension. This can be done in the following ways:

- Preface exposure to the **fumetto** or **fotoromanzo** with a preparatory activity that uses some of the main vocabulary to be acquired. For example, if the story introduces the theme of food and drink, bring in some real examples: bread rolls, cheese, ham, coffee, hot chocolate, water etc. Offer students something to eat or drink and encourage them to say what they like or don't like.

Once the mood has been set, write some key new words on the board. Students will then feel well set-up when they open their books to the **fumetto** or **fotoromanzo** and you switch on the tape. Many suggestions for such preparatory activities are contained in the Suggested Procedure section for each **capitolo** in this manual.

- Prepare the class for the **fumetto** or **fotoromanzo** by doing a selected exercise or two from the **In poche parole** or **A tu per tu** sections. These exercises have the advantage of focusing attention on a limited amount of language and the vocabulary thus acquired will shed light on significant parts of the story.

- Encourage intelligent guessing based on the photographs and illustrations and, where applicable, the students' familiarity with the characters.

- Set restricted comprehension targets that will give direction to each reading. You can concentrate on a specific vocabulary group or new language point. With each reading a new comprehension problem should be solved.

- Make well-timed use of the **Domande** in the *Textbook*. When you are doing these orally, allow students to give the simple, natural responses of spoken language rather than insisting on complete sentences. You can do that when they come to the comprehension exercises in the *Workbook*.

- Break the story into manageable sections which have a certain linguistic and/or thematic unity. In many cases it is appropriate to deal with the story a page at a time. In some cases, a single frame can provide the basis of a valuable language lesson.

- Have your students role-play sections of the story. They will read the character parts enthusiastically and readily imitate the pronunciation and intonation of the native-speaker performers on the *Cassettes*.

Constantly refer to the **fumetto** or **fotoromanzo** for examples of key language patterns: How did Maura ask...? What did Lucio say when...? If you give the lead by quoting or adapting phrases from the stories, your students will realise that they are an important source of useable language.

- Record a class performance of a story, encouraging students to adapt the script to suit their situation and to perform as much as possible without books in their hands.

Cultural information

There is no separate 'culture' section in *Forza!*, but the **fotoromanzi** and **fumetti** are rich in cultural content. Some, such as **Un giro di Roma con Antonio**, are explicitly 'cultural' in that they touch on key historical or geographical facts about Italy; most, however, carry information about life **all'italiana** more implicitly. In the case of **A casa con i Ferraro**, for example, students are given a window onto Italian family life, certain aspects of which are taken up in the **fumetto** entitled **La squadra Ferraro**.

Ideas for highlighting and following up the cultural content of the stories are contained in the Suggested Procedure section of each chapter of this manual. If there is sufficient time and interest, students could follow up class discussion with further research or project work.

Oral exercises and activities

Forza! rises to the challenge of giving students something to say, providing a wealth of visual material to stimulate a wide range of spoken responses. The *Forza!* method involves moving from highly structured, tightly focused exercises, **In poche parole**, through less structured exercises requiring increased learner input, **A tu per tu**, to relatively unstructured activities requiring practical use of the language, **A lingua sciolta!**

In poche parole

In general terms, the procedure for these exercises is to apply each cue-response box to each illustration or photograph. The parts of the dialogue to be varied are printed in bold. Where appropriate, the photos or illustrations are numbered for ease of reference. There are more detailed instructions on how to make **In poche parole** exercises work on page vi of the **Prefazione** to the *Textbook*.

From the teacher's point of view, the cue-response box brings into focus a particular language point for intensive oral practice. From the learner's perspective, each page provides a new piece of visual information that requires a range of considered responses. For the learner, the emphasis in the exercise is not on the language but on the information to be communicated. Focus is on meaning rather than form.

Before launching into an exercise, it will often be appropriate to spend some time setting the context for it with your students: Where are we? What are we looking at? What are we discussing? Why would we be saying that? Take, for example, exercise A on page 106 of the *Textbook*. You would set the scene in **Piazza Venezia** by checking its location on the map on page 185 and then looking again at the photos taken in this square on page 103. The **voglio** line could be spoken by someone driving a **motorino** in this heavy traffic, the **devi** line by a pillion passenger holding a map of Rome.

In poche parole exercises are suitable for use in the following formats: teacher – whole class; teacher – class section; teacher – student; student – whole class; student – class section; class section – class section; small group and pair work.

The most tightly structured way to handle these exercises is for you to give the cue for each picture in order and to demand a whole-class response in chorus. This approach will be very helpful early in the course, but you should be able to gradually wean students off the security of chorused responses to be more comfortable with some of the other formats.

As the class becomes more familiar with the language of a particular exercise, you should aim to make it progressively less teacher-centred. As soon as is practicable, let students take turns at giving the cues as well as the responses. Once they are confident with this they are ready to work in smaller class groupings and in pairs.

The most important stage in using the **In poche parole** exercises is to move away from the pictures on the page and to apply the language to your students' own lives. This move from a textbook-based exercise to a classroom-based activity (i.e. a conversation with students about their own lives) is vital. Your students will get the message that Italian is not about exercises in books but about using the language for real communication.

Since they isolate and highlight the important language points in each unit, you may elect to use selected **In poche parole** exercises as preparation for work on the **fotoromanzi** and **fumetti**.

A tu per tu

These pair-work dialogues take the next step towards a freer use of language by requiring more initiative on the part of students. The students have to combine the elements of language provided, or use the clues given by visual stimuli, to construct a coherent conversation. Working in pairs, they are asked to make a series of choices or substitutions which will eventually produce this coherence. Utterance follows thoughtful decision-making.

It is important to point out to students that the choices and substitutions they make have implications for later stages of the conversation they are in the process of building. If they make choices or substitutions that are inconsistent, the coherence of the conversation is lost. As the **Prefazione** to the *Textbook* points out to the students, 'It's no good if the other person tells you "Mi chiamo **Gino**" and you answer "Quanti anni hai, **Alessandro**?"'

You may choose to introduce these exercises by modelling a conversation with one of your more capable students, so that everyone in the class can see how to make it work. This sort of exercise does require concentration and students should be urged to persevere if things do not run smoothly at first. Those who are finding the going difficult could be directed to attempt the conversation a section at a time.

An invaluable by-product of the learner's involvement in this process will be a growing awareness of how discourse is constructed. These conversations can be used as frameworks around which students write dialogues of their own. Each pair of students will be only too pleased to perform their dialogue for the rest of the class!

A lingua sciolta!

The activities in this section offer students the most challenging and rewarding opportunity to put language acquired in each chapter to real communicative use.

A situation is suggested, a task is set, and students are expected to produce the appropriate language.

As far as oral work is concerned, the **A lingua sciolta!** activities in each chapter are critical. They test the student's ability to shed much of the scaffolding of the more structured exercises and to perform in a more realistic setting. This lack of structure can lead to a feeling that things are proceeding somewhat untidily and inconclusively, but it is important that students are encouraged to persevere and are positively reinforced in their efforts.

The first step in setting the task is to make sure that students clearly understand what is required of them. Once the task is understood it is essential to ensure that the necessary language has been clearly grasped by your students. This will probably involve revision of some key language points dealt with in the chapter. Although these are obviously not teacher-centred activities, teacher support and monitoring will play a big part in their eventual success. Not all of the scaffolding disappears!

Try to make the situations as realistic as possible by using appropriate props and other realia. Even a minimal attempt to ensure that students have something extra to wear, hold or point to will add to their level of interest and involvement. Do not hesitate to rearrange your classroom to create a more realistic setting.

Your approach to the assessment of the activities is also crucial. If your students are communicating effectively in the course of the activity, you can reserve your corrections until they have completed it. Continual interruptions can inhibit students at a stage where it is best to encourage fluency and to boost confidence. While you will be aiming for a high standard, you will be aware that unstructured oral interaction is the most difficult language skill to master. Your expectations need to be realistic, your comments encouraging.

Where materials such as survey forms are required for an activity, they appear as repromasters in the relevant chapters of this manual.

Studiamo la lingua!

Forza! is not a grammar-driven course. It is *topic-based*, in the sense that the focus of each chapter is the area of experience that it deals with – school, family, leisure etc. – and the language that is needed to communicate effectively in that context. It is also *activity-based*, in the sense that the primary aim of each chapter is to enable students to perform specified communicative tasks rather than to come to a notional understanding of certain grammar points.

Within this framework, grammar does retain an important role. Its purpose is to organise experience of the language so that patterns emerging from one situation can be applied in another. The presentation of grammar in *Forza!* is carefully integrated with the language of the **fotoromanzi** and **fumetti** and the various exercises throughout each chapter. It is important, however, that you do not communicate that this chapter is 'about plurals' or that in this chapter 'we are doing the **-are** verbs'.

Since the **Studiamo la lingua!** section provides a convenient overview of the language points dealt with in each chapter, some teachers will consult it before plunging into the various exercises and activities that precede it. From the learner's point of view, however, it is important that the language in each chapter is introduced in concrete form. Students need to experience the language in action, and they do this by becoming actively involved in the exercises and activities throughout the chapter. As a result of this experience, they should be in a position to help you make some useful statements about how the language works.

One of the most difficult things is to judge when the moment has come to launch into an organised summary of language points and to decide how detailed your grammatical explanations should be. Some of your students will find that such explanations provide useful insights into how the language works, others will find them confusing. This is very much a matter of the teacher's sensitive response to the needs of a particular class and to individuals within the class.

As the Contents pages make clear, the second

half of *Forza! uno* pays attention to the reinforcement of already practised language points as well as the introduction of new ones. This constant recycling of language means that allowance is made for a gradual coming-to-terms with how Italian works so that students do not have to have a perfect grasp of one chapter before they can move on to the next.

In summary, then:

- Don't start the teaching of a language point in the abstract. Start with concrete situations and use the grammar as a way of organising the language experience.

- Try to gauge the readiness of students for grammatical explanations and be ready to cater for individual differences.

- Don't dictate the rules, let your students help you formulate them.

- Allow for understanding to develop gradually.

- Don't allow work on grammar to dominate your method. See it as a means to a communicative end.

Impariamo le parole!

Learning the words is a primary task of the language student. Much of this can happen incidentally as students are exposed to the language in the **fumetti** and **fotoromanzi** and the various exercises and activities throughout the course. However, if you rely entirely on the absorption method you will be amazed at the ability of some of your students not to acquire key words and expressions, no matter how vigorous and imaginative your presentation has been. Regular rote-learning and testing of vocabulary is the best way of overcoming this sort of imperviousness.

To this end, the **Impariamo le parole!** section at the conclusion of each story is divided into manageable blocks having some sort of grammatical or topic-related unity. You can set your students the task of regularly learning a block of vocabulary with the expectation that this will be tested in class. This routine can, of course, be readily converted into some sort of competitive game.

The **Impariamo le parole!** sections contain the active vocabulary of the *Forza! uno* course. These are the words and expressions your students are expected to acquire and to use in exercises and activities. There is also some passive vocabulary, most notably in the various authentic materials throughout the book. These words and expressions are included for comprehension only and are contained in the word list at the back of the *Textbook*.

Workbook

While the *Texbook* is all 'colour and movement', the *Workbook* provides students with the space to work quietly away at all the language they have been listening to and speaking in class. From the outset, they should be encouraged to value this book, to look after it and to write in it with care. After all, it will be their main working space for a long time!

The *Workbook* contains the following sections: **Su con l'orecchio!**, **Penna in mano!**, **Studiamo la lingua!** and **Rompicapi**.

Su con l'orecchio!

Under the **Su con l'orecchio!** heading you will find the listening comprehension exercises for each chapter. The tape scripts for the exercises are in this manual in the Suggested Procedure section of each chapter.

In many of these **Su con l'orecchio!** exercises the specific comprehension point being tested is often located in a wealth of surrounding language. In the first instance, instruct your students to listen for the specific comprehension targets. Once these have been reached you can return to the passages to exploit some of the other language. The Suggested Procedure section for each chapter often provides supplementary questions to help focus attention on this surrounding language.

One of the most useful teaching aids in this part of the course is the pause button on your cassette recorder. You will also find many occasions to make the most of the rewind facility on the machine. There is no need to throw the class on the mercy of the recorded voices: you're in charge, you set the pace.

Of course, you will not restrict the teaching of listening comprehension skills to the **Su con l'orecchio!** exercises. You will seize every opportunity to let your students hear Italian

spoken as you work the ever increasing fund of Italian words and expressions into everyday life in the classroom.

More specific hints for the use of the **Su con l'orecchio!** exercises are to be found in this manual, in the Suggested Procedure section of each chapter.

Penna in mano!

The first set of exercises under the **Penna in mano!** heading consists of reading comprehension exercises based on the **fotoromanzi** and **fumetti**.

Some of these are **Vero o falso?** questions which are intended as a quick and effective means of clarifying the meaning of the text. Sometimes, however, they can lead to debate, especially where an opinion is called for. Rather than being frustrated by the lack of a clear correct answer, take consolation from the fact that in order to argue the point, students have to understand the story.

Sometimes the comprehension exercises take the form of **Domande** to be answered in complete sentences. Since they test a writing skill as well as comprehension, students will need careful preparation for them. You may need to continually remind them of the meanings of the different interrogatives they have met and the sort of answer that each one calls for: **Chi?** means your answer will mention a person, **Dove?** calls for a place, etc.

Early in your treatment of the **fotoromanzo** or **fumetto** you can deal with these questions orally, concentrating on *assisting* students with their understanding. You can then follow up with the written exercises in the *Workbook* where your emphasis can be more on *assessing* how well they have understood the text.

Lettere

In most chapters there is a letter-writing activity, the aim of which is to stress the importance of writing as a form of communication. Students write to the characters they meet in the **fotoromanzi**, to the Rome tourist authority, to the Nintendo company and to **Babbo Natale** or **la Befana**.

In preparation for these activities you will have

to gauge the amount of pre-teaching and/or revision required, and then help students plan their writing. Some of the tasks are quite challenging and you will achieve the best results when you support students in the initial stages.

When you are assessing the work produced in this section you can apply the positive criteria you use in evaluating creative writing. Don't discourage your budding authors by focusing exclusively on errors of grammar or spelling. Reward those who discover inventive ways of showing that the language they are learning can be used in real communication. Make the better efforts available to the rest of the class so that everyone can appreciate what is possible.

The chapter-by-chapter teacher's notes include a sample letter where appropriate, as an indication of the type and standard of writing your students can aim for. You can use these samples to help convince students that they *do* have the language to complete the tasks that have been set. They are presented as repromasters, so that a poster, overhead transparency or photocopies can be made as appropriate.

Rompicapi

The **Rompicapi** section contains a variety of word games and puzzles which allow students to have some fun with the new words and expressions they are learning. The word puzzles and crossword in each chapter pick up some of the more incidental vocabulary and will be useful revision instruments if held off until the end of the final stage.

Assistance with sequencing the various puzzles in relation to the other exercises and activities is given in the chapter-by-chapter notes in the *Teacher's Manual*.

Teacher's Manual

The *Forza! uno Teacher's Manual* is divided into eight chapters, based on the divisions of the *Textbook*. Each chapter contains the following sections: Suggested Procedure, Suggested Assessment Tasks, **Su con l'orecchio!** Tape Scripts, *Forza! uno* Student Progress Sheets. Repromasters are provided in the relevant chapters.

Suggested procedure

The observations and suggestions in the Suggested Procedure section of each chapter form the nucleus of this manual. They tackle the task of sequencing the many and varied exercises and activities and offer practical hints for their day-to-day implementation in the classroom.

The Suggested Procedure is presented in stages, each stage having a certain thematic and/or linguistic unity. The language of this section may appear to be quite directive at times but the suggested procedures are just that, suggestions. It is not the place of this manual to be prescriptive; what it can do is clarify the intentions of the author and offer one approach that will work. In many cases, what is written in the manual will trigger an idea for a creative departure from the Suggested Procedure.

Suggested assessment tasks

There are no official end-of-chapter tests in this manual. What is suggested is a number of exercises and activities that can be used as common assessment tasks, in a way that makes assessment an integral part of the on-going teaching and learning process.

This 'assessment package' system allows teachers to design tests that take into account the particular experience of an individual class. This may involve supplementing exercises and activities from the course with test items of your own making.

Su con l'orecchio! tape scripts

Having the **Su con l'orecchio!** Tape Scripts will assist you in the preparation of the listening comprehension exercises in that you will be able to foresee any potential problems and take appropriate action. This may take the form of some pre-teaching, revision or preparatory conversation.

Once students have achieved the primary objectives of the **Su con l'orecchio!** exercises, you can use these scripts to do further work on their aural comprehension. They are also available for use as sample dialogues, for reading comprehension, dictation or even translation.

Forza! uno student progress sheets

The Student Progress Sheets state the objectives of each chapter in terms of communication tasks, and include columns for recording an assessment of the student's progress towards achieving these objectives. This can include a self-evaluation, an evaluation made by a classmate and a confirmation or correction of these to be made by the teacher. The system used to record these evaluations will be a matter for decision by the teacher or negotiation with the class.

Since they set the targets for the chapter these sheets are ideal for distribution at the beginning of each new unit of work. After some initial discussion, each student then holds a document that gives direction to the work done in class. The sheet can also be used at any stage to check an individual's progress.

Learning how to learn

The aims of this section of the course are:

- to make students aware of the nature and the role of language and its relationship to culture; and

- to help students to develop attitudes and strategies that will lead to effective language-learning as well as a sense of personal responsibility for that learning.

The Learning How to Learn section is intended as a basis for class discussion in which students can air the problems they are having and share strategies for overcoming them. Since the material in this section is not necessarily tied to the language covered in a particular chapter, it is presented in the form of repromasters which you can introduce whenever you like.

Cassettes

The *Forza! uno Cassettes* contain recordings of the **fotoromanzi** and **fumetti** from the *Textbook,* as well as the **Su con l'orecchio!** exercises from the *Workbook.*

Suggested procedure

STAGE 1

• *Preparatory activity 1*

If the class arrives at the room before you do you could make a great show of wondering whether you have come to the right place: **Questa è la mia classe? Sì, questa è la mia classe!** You could announce to startled passers-by in the corridor: **Questa è la mia classe!**

Make your first direct contact with your new class in Italian. If your students stand at the beginning of a new lesson you could begin by giving a gesture-supported direction: **In piedi, per favore.** You then greet the class with a simple **buongiorno.** Persevere through the nervous giggles and comments until the class has returned your greeting to your satisfaction. If they have been standing, you could gesture them into their seats: **Sedetevi, per favore.**

If there are students that you know well, you could wave to one or two with a cheery **Ciao, Craig! Ciao, Louise!**

• *Preparatory activity 2*

With the help of extravagant gestures, introduce yourself to people in your class: **Mi chiamo Michele.** Move straight into the question **Come ti chiami?** Once they have the idea and answer satisfactorily, reward them with a friendly greeting: **Ciao, Anita. Buongiorno, Jamie.**

You could consolidate at this early stage by writing on the board: **Buongiorno. Ciao. Mi chiamo.** Ask the students to write in their exercise books the greeting they feel like using and then their name.

• *Preparatory activity 3*

The final preparation for the material in the *Textbook* could take the form of some introductions of one student to another: **Rebecca, questo è Josh. (Ciao, Josh.) Josh, questa è Rebecca. (Ciao, Rebecca.)**

• *Questa è la mia classe* Textbook p 2

Prepare the class for your first reading of the **fotoromanzo** entitled **Questa è la mia classe,** by telling them that they will hear people introducing themselves and their friends, saying how old they are and where they live. They are not expected to understand it all perfectly; they can concentrate on getting to know the new characters. You could add a couple of general comprehension questions: Who is the oldest? How old? What are two words (almost the same) used for 'friend'?

After your first reading, discuss answers to these questions and any other immediate comprehension difficulties class members are anxious about. In some cases you will ask them to be patient: they will be coming back to this story several times. You could also tell them that the **fotoromanzo** is continued in the **fumetto** later in the chapter.

• *In poche parole 1A* Textbook p 6

The emphasis in this exercise is on getting to know the characters and practising greetings. For this first exercise, you give all the cues and have the class respond as a whole.

▲ Questa è **Alessia.**
■ Ciao, **Alessia**!

Can students work out why you sometimes say **questo** while at other times you say **questa**?

• *Concluding activity 4*

At the end of the lesson reassure your students that you will be seeing one another again: **Arrivederci!** They will understand that they are free to go once they have returned your farewell greeting to your satisfaction. The students you greeted earlier with a cheery **Ciao!** will appreciate a more informal farewell: **Ciao, Craig! Ciao, Louise!**

STAGE 2

• *Preparatory activity 1*

Begin each lesson by greeting your class collectively and individually. If you have not already done so, ask students to add **signore** or **signora**.

If a lesson happens to be towards the end of the

school day you could wonder aloud: **È buongiorno o buonasera?** Another way to introduce **buonasera** would be to set up a student to come in late. Your little rehearsed dialogue would go something like this:

▲ **Permesso, signora?**
■ **Avanti! Avanti!**

▲ **Buongiorno, signora.**
■ **È buongiorno o buonasera?** (*Point to watch*) **Guarda! Sei in ritardo.**

Ask how many in the class have understood the difference between **buongiorno** and **buonasera**. Students could copy **buonasera** into their notebooks where they have been writing down the greetings.

Summarise your work on this section by discussing and explaining when you use these greetings: **ciao, buongiorno, buonasera, arrivederci.**

• *Penna in mano! A Saluti*
Workbook p 4

Check that your students know what to look for in the illustrations. Are they meeting or parting? What time of day is it? Is it a formal or informal situation?

• *Su con l'orecchio! A Saluti*
Workbook p 1, Cassette 3, tape script Teacher's Manual, p 6

Prepare your class for their first listening comprehension exercise by making sure they understand exactly what is required of them. Be ready to use the pause button and to replay items whenever you think this is necessary.

• *Preparatory activity 2*

Go back to asking the names of the students who have not yet introduced themselves. Then start asking **Chi è questo?** Someone will understand what you are after and tell you **Questo è Tran.** Once you are satisfied that you have practised this enough, you could write masculine and feminine examples of the question and answer on the board for students to copy into their books.

• *Questa è la mia classe* Textbook p 2

Reacquaint your class with the story and the characters by listening to and reading the **fotoromanzo** for a second time.

• *In poche parole 1B* Textbook p 6

Once you are happy with the way the class is handling the responses, you could have students perform this exercise in pairs, taking it in turns to test each other on their knowledge of the characters.

• *Su con l'orecchio! B Chi è?*
Workbook p 1, Cassette 3, tape script Teacher's Manual p 6

In this exercise, students will hear **si chiama** for the first time. It is there for passive comprehension, not yet for active use. There is no need to explain it unless a student draws attention to it.

The number students write under the pictures is, of course, the number of the item within the exercise, as announced on the tape. They may not know the numbers in Italian yet, so you could either teach them 1–10 now, or let them work out that the exercise starts at 1 and goes through to 7. You can correct this exercise as soon as the class has completed it.

• *Penna in mano! B Chi è?*
Workbook p 5

Take the opportunity to encourage students to write neatly in their workbooks – they have to last a long time. Ask them to use some common sense in tailoring the size of their handwriting to the space available.

STAGE 3

• *Preparatory activity 1*

Be alert to opportunities to use the exclamations and the other expressions that occur in this chapter: **Forza! Andiamo! Permesso? Avanti! Guarda! Mi dispiace! Scusa! In piedi! Sedetevi! Silenzio! Uffa! Va bene!** You should be able to work several of these into your classroom language every lesson. Encourage your students to use them as well.

• *Preparatory activity 2*

For a change of pace, teach your students to count from 1 to 20. Have them count after you, then together as a class. Introduce variations such as counting by twos and counting backwards. Go around the class in an agreed order and have individuals say the correct number when it comes to their turn. **I numeri** are set out on page 5 of the *Textbook*.

• *Game: Ciao!*

After students have practised saying the correct number when it comes to their turn, they are ready to play **Ciao!** (Buzz!).

First, go around the class just having individuals say the numbers. Anyone who makes a mistake or hesitates unduly is out. You then decide that you will say **Ciao!** instead of certain numbers, for example 6 and 13. Anyone who forgets and says the number is out. The rule about mistakes and hesitations still applies. Keep adding to or changing the **Ciao!** numbers until you have a winner.

• *Rompicapi A Più o meno*
  Workbook p 12

This puzzle gives some practice at writing numbers in words.

Solution: The mystery sentence is **Ha cento anni.**

• *Studiamo la lingua! C Che numero hai? Workbook p 2*

In this exercise the *Forza!* characters receive their locker numbers for the year. In the first instance, let the class concentrate on connecting the characters with their lockers. You could follow this exercise by playing the tape again and setting some more general comprehension targets:

1 Why is the teacher a bit cross with Claudio?
2 What number is Laura desperate not to have?
3 What number does Scarno want? Why can't he have it?

Return to Laura's anxiety about 17. You could explain that 17 is regarded (by some) as an unlucky number in Italy. Italians are generally aware that people in other countries are superstitious about 13, so some have transferred their worries about 17 to 13. Many, probably most, Italians are not superstitious at all and do not associate numbers with good or bad luck.

• *Questa è la mia classe Textbook p 2*
Listen to and read the story again. Alessia refers to her class as **la seconda media**. You could briefly

explain to the class how this year level fits into the Italian school system, tailoring the amount of detail to the interest shown by your class.

After a year or two at **asilo** (**scuola materna**) between the ages of three and five, Italian children go to **scuola elementare** for five years. After that they attend **scuola media** for three years, so **seconda media** is roughly equivalent to Year 7 or 8. The next stage of schooling, senior high school, is called **liceo**. There are different types of **liceo**, concentrating on different types of courses, so students can choose which one to go to according to their interests. If they would rather not attend an academic senior high, students can choose a more job-oriented **istituto professionale**.

• *In poche parole 1C Textbook p 6*
Note that **Come si chiama?** does not occur in the **fotoromanzo**, so this exercise *presents* as well as *practises* this language point. You could underline the difference between it and **Come ti chiami?** by writing both on the board.

• *Penna in mano! C Vero o falso?*
  Workbook p 5

Before students start this reading comprehension exercise, make sure they understand the expression **abita a...** Look briefly at the photos of Rome included in the **fotoromanzo** and explain what is depicted there. This is just a fleeting glimpse. The class will get to know Rome much better as the course progresses!

STAGE 4

• *Preparatory activity 1*
It is high time that you practised **Come stai?** with your class. Go around to individuals, revise the greetings they know and extend to asking how they are. Someone will remember **Bene, grazie** and **Non c'è male** from the **fotoromanzo**. You can remind them about **E tu?** as you go from one class member to another. Be pleased rather than offended if they say **E tu?** to you. There is time enough to learn the **Lei** form at a later stage.

• *Preparatory activity 2*
Having established that everyone is well you could move on to model the sort of self-introduction towards which your class is working:

Mi chiamo Michele. Ho venticinque anni. Abito a Clifton Hill.

Extract similar information from your students: **E tu, come ti chiami? Quanti anni hai? Dove abiti?**

Let them hear the third person: **Dunque, Kristen abita a Clifton East. E tu?**

• *Informazioni personali*
  Workbook title page

Your students are well placed to fill in this information sheet. They may need to be reminded of the meaning of **la mia scuola** and **la mia classe**.

• *Questa è la mia classe* Textbook p 2

Take advantage of this third run through the **fotoromanzo** to iron out any remaining comprehension problems.

• *In poche parole 2* Textbook p 7

Students are not required to speak to the characters depicted in the *Textbook*, as this might strike them as an unnatural thing to do. Practising the first and third persons is usually done in the classroom activities and the **A tu per tu** exercises. You may decide, however, that you need to practise the first and second persons in the context of a more structured oral exercise. In that case you could precede the dialogues in the *Textbook* with the following:

A ▲ Come ti chiami?
2 ■ Mi chiamo **Ambra**.

B ▲ Quanti anni hai?
2 ■ Ho **quattro** anni.

C ▲ Dove abiti?
2 ■ Abito a **Napoli**.

• *Penna in mano! D Anni e abitazione* Workbook p 6

• *Su con l'orecchio! D Dove abiti? Quanti anni hai?* Workbook p 2, Cassette 3, tape script Teacher's Manual p 7

Notice that after the interviewer thanks a couple of the young people interviewed, they respond with **Prego**. Ask students what they think it means in this context.

• *Penna in mano! E Come si chiama? Quanti anni ha? Dove abita?* Workbook p 7

• *A tu per tu* Textbook p 14

This is probably the first time your students have done an exercise like this, so they will need to have it explained to them quite thoroughly. Stress the need to listen to the choices their partner makes so that they can respond accordingly: it doesn't make much sense for the partner to choose the name Alessandro and then be addressed as Gino (much less Gina!).

It may be an idea for you to do this exercise (or a part of it) with a few students and then have a couple of students perform it for the benefit of the whole class. You will need to set a high standard for pair-work exercises and activities since your students will be required to do many of them as the course progresses.

• *Penna in mano! F Questa è l'Italia* Workbook p 8

This map exercise is intended as a most general introduction to the geography of Italy with a quick look at some principal cities. You could introduce the divisions of north, centre and south. You could ask:

1 Which city would you call a northern city?
2 What about **Firenze**?
3 Are there any people in the class from Italy?
4 Where on the map is their city/town/village?

STAGE 5

• *Che ore sono?* Textbook p 8

It would be good to introduce this topic by timing things so that you can point to the classroom clock and exclaim **Sono le dieci!** (You could always fix things by taking the batteries out of the clock or by bringing in one that you have stopped on the hour.) You could then expect a correct answer when you ask **Che ore sono?** You can then move with confidence to the *Textbook* exercise.

• *Su con l'orecchio! E Che ore sono?* Workbook p 3, Cassette 3, tape script Teacher's Manual p 7

Tell your students that they will hear things other than the time. They are not expected to understand every word but to listen for the information they require.

- **Rompicapi C Guarda!** *Workbook p 13*

Solution: The letters left over in this puzzle spell **Sei in ritardo**.

- **Scarno fa la seconda media** *Textbook p 10*

This **fumetto** should help consolidate the language you have been dealing with in this chapter and to prepare students for the oral and written activities to follow. Having read and listened to the story, have students role-play the different character parts.

- **Su con l'orecchio! F Questo è il mio amico** *Workbook p 3, Cassette 3, tape script Teacher's Manual p 8*

This listening exercise revises introductions and prepares the class for the activities to follow.

- **Penna in mano! H Questo è il mio amico** *Workbook p 9*

A written follow-up to the listening exercise above.

- **A lingua sciolta! 1 Buongiorno!** *Textbook p 15*

Stress to your students that this is the most important activity they have done for the whole chapter. It shows that they can use their Italian in a real situation and not rely on working from a book. To help increase their confidence, it is probably best to have students prepare their 'speech' at home.

From your point of view, this activity is the most effective way of assessing your students' progress with the language. Don't forget to be positive in your assessment, congratulating them on what they do well rather than focusing on their mistakes. Insist that classmates be equally encouraging.

- **Rompicapi B Troviamo le parole!** *Workbook p 12*

Solution: The left-over letters spell **Silenzio!**

- **A lingua sciolta! 2 Dove abiti?** *Textbook p 15*

The talkfest continues. You may decide to have this as an alternative to the previous activity. Since it is more substantial and challenging, you may have to encourage some students to choose this second activity. The interview segment should be performed publicly.

- **Su con l'orecchio! G Forza!** *Workbook p 4, Cassette 3, tape script Teacher's Manual p 8*

Make sure your students understand clearly what is required of them. For each conversation they need to write a number in two boxes.

- **Penna in mano! I Cosa dire?** *Workbook p 10*

Before you have students begin this exercise, satisfy yourself that they have sufficient exposure to the expressions they are required to use here. If, for example, you feel that they have not seen and heard **Mi dispiace!** enough, contrive a situation in which an apology is required. You could, for example, mistake someone's name or arrive late for class.

- **Penna in mano! J Quante domande!** *Workbook p 11*

This exercise is framed the way it is to give it a functional tone, thus avoiding the non-functional feel of straight translation. This does lead to some anomolous wording at times, as in the reference to 'this person'. This is just a way of requiring students to use the third person forms they know.

- **Penna in mano! K Andiamo a Roma** *Workbook p 11*

This activity may strain credibility just a little, but there is an attempt to give a sense of purpose to this very simple writing task. It is important, even at this very early stage, that your students see that writing in Italian can be directed to a specified 'audience' with some practical outcomes.

You could insist that this is a genuine competition and that you will be forwarding the best entries on to Rome. You could also display your students' efforts around the classroom and use stickers, postcards or posters as encouragement awards.

Suggested assessment tasks

Listening

- **Su con l'orecchio! D Dove abiti? Quanti anni hai?** *Workbook p 2,*

Cassette 3, tape script Teacher's Manual p 7

- **Su con l'orecchio! E Che ore sono?** *Workbook p 3, tape script Teacher's Manual p 7*
- **Su con l'orecchio! F Questo è il mio amico** *Workbook p 3, Cassette 3, tape script Teacher's Manual p 8*

Speaking

- **In poche parole 2** *Textbook p 7*
- **Che ore sono?** *Textbook p 8*
- **A tu per tu** *Textbook p 14*
- **A lingua sciolta! 2 Dove abiti?** *Textbook p 15*

Reading

- **Penna in mano! C Vero o falso?** *Workbook p 5*

Writing

- **Penna in mano! B Chi è?** *Workbook p 5*
- **Penna in mano! E Come si chiama? Quanti anni ha? Dove abita?** *Workbook p 7*
- **Penna in mano! J Quante domande!** *Workbook p 11*
- **Penna in mano! K Andiamo a Roma!** *Workbook p 11*

Su con l'orecchio! Tape scripts

A Saluti

Listen to these brief conversations and highlight the greeting you hear. If you hear two greetings, mark them both.

1 – Buongiorno, signora.
  – Ah, buongiorno, Claudio. Come stai?
  – Bene, grazie, signora.

2 – Ciao, Maria-Chiara.
  – Ciao, Alessia. Come stai?
  – Be', non c'è male. E tu?

3 – Arrivederci, ragazzi.

– Arrivederci, signora.

4 – Ciao, Alessia! Ciao, Laura!
  – Ciao, Maria-Chiara! Arrivederci!

5 – Buonasera, signora.
  – Buonasera, Scarno.

6 – Permesso, signora?
  – Avanti, Dario. È buongiorno o buonasera, ragazzi?
  – È buonasera, è buonasera. Dario è in ritardo.

B Chi è?

A couple of Alessia's teachers are getting to know the **seconda media** students by looking at photos of them. When you have worked out who they are talking about, write the number under the photo.

1 – Chi è questa?
  – Questa è Alessia.
  – Alessia fa la seconda media?
  – Sì, sì. Ha dodici anni.
  – Dodici anni!! Mamma mia!

2 – E questo, chi è?
  – È Dario.
  – Ah, Dario. Lui è sempre in ritardo, no?
  – No, non sempre.

3 – Ah, questo è l'amico di Dario. Si chiama Rino, no?
  – No, si chiama Claudio.
  – Ah, sì, sì, sì. Claudio.

4 – E questa, chi è?
  – È Laura. Laura è l'amica di Alessia.
  – Laura è di Milano, no?
  – Sì, ma adesso abita qui a Roma.

5 – Questo qui si chiama Roberto, no?
  – Sì, sì, è Roberto.

6 – E lei? Maria-Teresa?
  – No, Maria-Chiara. Maria-Chiara è un'amica di Alessia.

7 – Mamma mia! Questo, chi è? Anche lui fa la seconda media?
  – Sì, anche lui fa la seconda media. Si chiama Scarno. Scarno è un amico di Roberto.

C Che numero hai?

The teacher is giving out locker numbers to the **seconda media** students. Draw a line to connect the people with the locker they have been given.

1 – Roberto, il numero 4.

2 – Maria-Chiara, tu hai il numero 12.

3 – Alessia, prendi il 14. Va bene?
  – 14 va benissimo, signora.

4 – Claudio, 19.
  – Numero 9, signora?
  – No, Claudio. 19. Sta' attento!
  – Sì, signora. Mi dispiace, signora.

5 – Laura, tu prendi il numero 17.
  – No, signora. Per favore, non il 17.
  – Va bene, prendi il 15.
  – Grazie, signora.

6 – Dario, il numero 10.
  – Grazie, signora.

7 – Scarno, c'è l'uno e c'è il 20. Quale preferisci?
  – Non c'è il numero 100, signora?
  – No, il 100 non c'è.
  – Va bene, il numero 20, signora.
  – Scarno, 20.

D Dove abiti? Quanti anni hai?

A reporter is interviewing young people in the streets of Rome. Write their age next to their name and then draw a line to connect them with the city they live in.

1 – Buongiorno. Come ti chiami?
  – Mi chiamo Grazia.
  – Quanti anni hai, Grazia?
  – Ho undici anni.
  – Undici anni? Brava! E dove abiti?
  – Abito a Firenze.
  – Firenze! Che bella città! Grazie, Grazia.
  – Prego.

2 – Ti chiami?
  – Antonio. Mi chiamo Antonio.
  – Ciao, Antonio. Dimmi, quanti anni hai?
  – Ho tredici anni.
  – Tredici anni. Grazie. E abiti...?
  – Io abito a Palermo.

– Ah, un siciliano. Grazie, Antonio di Palermo.
  – Prego.

3 – Buonasera. Come ti chiami?
  – Mi chiamo Rinaldi Renato.
  – Renato. Un bel nome. Quanti anni hai, Renato?
  – Ho diciassette anni.
  – E abiti qui a Roma?
  – No, abito a Milano.
  – Ah, Milano. È una bella città.
  – Eh, sì, non c'è male.

4 – Buonasera.
  – Buonasera.
  – Stai bene?
  – Molto bene, grazie.
  – Ti chiami Tina, no?
  – No, mi chiamo Santina.
  – Scusa, Santina, mi dispiace. Dimmi, quanti anni hai?
  – Ho quattordici anni.
  – E dove abiti, Santina?
  – Abito a Napoli.
  – Ah, una bella napoletana. Grazie, Santina.

5 – Scusa, come ti chiami?
  – Mi chiamo Massimo.
  – Quanti anni hai, Massimo?
  – Ho quindici anni.
  – E abiti qui a Roma?
  – Sì, abito qui a Roma. Sono romano.
  – Grazie.
  – Prego. Arrivederci.

E Che ore sono?

Listen for the time and draw a line to show it on the sundials.

1 – Scusa, che ore sono?
  – Guarda, sono le sei.

2 – Che ore sono, per favore?
  – Sono le nove.
  – Le nove precise?
  – Le nove precise.

3 – Mamma mia, sono le otto!!! Ciao. Arrivederci.
  – Ciao, Dario. Poveretto, è sempre in ritardo.

4 – Buongiorno.
 – Buongiorno?!? Sono le sette di sera.
 – Le sette? Buonasera, allora.

5 – Scusa, che ore sono?
 – Sono le dodici e...Ecco! È l'una.

6 – Sono le cinque! Forza! Andiamo!
 – O.K.! O.K.! Sono le cinque. Sono pronto.

F Questo è il mio amico

Listen to these people introducing their friends and draw a line to connect them.

1 – Ciao. Mi chiamo Alessia, e questa è la mia amica Laura.

2 – Buongiorno. Io mi chiamo Roberto, e questo è il mio amico Scarno.

3 – Io sono Maria-Chiara, e questa è la mia amica Olivia.

4 – Questo è il mio amico Renzo. Ah sì, scusa! Io mi chiamo Dario.

5 – Ciao. Io sono Claudio, e questa è la mia amica Gabriella.

6 – Io mi chiamo Alessandra e questo è il mio amico Gino.

G Forza!

You will hear two of these expressions used in each of these brief conversations. Write the number in the appropriate boxes.

1 – Silenzio, ragazzi! Silenzio...Uffa!

2 – Permesso, signora?
 – Avanti, Dario. Avanti.

3 – Sono le otto. Forza! Andiamo! Forza!

4 – Avanti, Laura. Avanti, Santina. Sedetevi.

5 – Scusa, che ore sono?
 – Guarda, sono le dieci.

6 – Signora, mi chiamo Maria-Chiara, non Maria-Luisa.
 – Va bene, Maria-Chiara. Mi dispiace.

Forza! uno student progress sheet

In the **io** column, give yourself a tick for each thing that you know how to do in Italian. Then ask a friend to check you and mark the **amico/a** column. Keep the last column free for when your teacher has time to hear how you are progressing.

Nome _____ **Classe** _____

Capitolo 1	io	amico/a	
Give an appropriate greeting			
Ask how someone is			
Say how you are			
Ask someone's name			
Give your own name			
Ask someone's age			
Give your own age			
Ask where someone lives			
Say where you live			
Introduce yourself			
Introduce someone else			
Ask what time it is			
Tell the time (on the hour)			
Ask permission to come in			
Tell someone to come in			
Tell people to sit down			
Tell people to be quiet			
Encourage people to go on			
Apologise for being late			
Count to 20			
Name five important Italian cities			

Capitolo ② Ti piace?

Suggested procedure

STAGE 1

- *Preparatory activity 1*

Run an eye over the adjectives to be used in this chapter and see if you can introduce a few in the context of your classroom. You could look for the student wearing track shoes or some other item of sportswear: **Ah, Connie, tu sei sportiva.** Make a show of being strict: **Silenzio! Silenzio, ragazzi! Io sono severo, no?** Lavish praise upon the modest achievers: **Bravo, Jordan! Tu sei molto bravo in italiano. Brava, Sarah! Sei molto intelligente.**

- *Ti piace? Textbook p 18*

Prepare your class for their first reading of the **fotoromanzo** by telling them that they will be meeting a different set of **seconda media** students. This time the class will see and hear a number of words that the students use about themselves and others to say what they are like. Ask your students what we call these describing words.

People in your class may comment on the racial mix they will notice in the two Roman classrooms they have seen. You could explain that Italy has had a connection with Africa since its colonising days (not to mention the days of Hannibal!) and that there is quite a strong African presence in Rome and some of the other big cities.

After you have read and listened to the **fotoromanzo** tell your class that the story is continued in the **fumetto** later in the chapter.

- *Penna in mano! A Chi è? Com'è? Workbook p 18*

This exercise gives your students a chance to familiarise themselves with the new characters and vocabulary of this early part of the chapter. The new grammatical element is the third person pronoun, **lui/lei**, which is used to emphasise 'he' or 'she' (as in **anche lei...**)

- *Su con l'orecchio! A Chi è? Workbook p 14, Cassette 3, tape script Teacher's Manual p 15*

- *In poche parole 1A Textbook p 22*

- *Penna in mano! B È molto intelligente Workbook p 19*

There is scope in this exercise for your students to express opinions that will not be shared by everyone else in the class. Sometimes they will feel that they can't be expected to know (e.g. whether Antonella is intelligent or not). As a general rule they should accept what has been said in the text, unless there is evidence to contradict it. Any divergence of opinion should be welcome, as long as it is correctly expressed!

You will need to explain how to say that someone is not... (The explanation in the *Textbook* occurs on page 35, following a partial presentation of the verb **essere**.) Sometimes a student will see a chance to go further than a simple expression of a negative: **No, non è antipatica, è simpatica. No, non è birichino, è timido.**

A brief explanation of **molto** will also be needed for students who want to say that someone is very...

- *In poche parole 1B Textbook p 23*

For a first run-through, you may decide to ask the class to respond in unison so that they can build up confidence handling **molto** with the adjectives and then the negative construction with **non**. In that case, you will need to ask a series of questions that sit well with affirmative answers, followed by a series requiring negative answers.

Affirmative:

1 **Lidia è sportiva?**
2 **Antonella è intelligente?**
3 **Barbara è spiritosa?**
4 **La signora Gallicani è severa?**
5 **Adriano è timido?**
6 **Elena è alta?**
7 **Giorgio è spiritoso?**

Negative:

8 **Angela è brava in basket?**
9 **Antonella è alta?**

10 **Barbara è timida?**

11 **La signora Gallicani è antipatica?**

12 **Adriano è spiritoso?**

13 **Elena è brutta?**

14 **Giorgio è timido?**

It is important to go on to give students some practice at asking the questions as well as giving the answers.

STAGE 2

• *Preparatory activity*

Try to find an opportunity to state a couple of likes. If there is a basketball or tennis racquet in the room you could handle them lovingly: **Mi piace il basket/tennis.** Pause after the musical introduction to the **fotoromanzo** entitled **Mi piace la musica.** You could ask one of your students: **Ti piace la musica, Siobhan?** Reflect warmly on the performance of your students: **Mi piace questa classe. Questa classe è molto intelligente!**

• *Ti piace?* Textbook p 18

You could tell your students to listen particularly for the characters in the story talking about people and things they like. Encourage them to ask questions to help clear up any remaining comprehension questions.

• *In poche parole 1C* Textbook p 23

This exercise affords an opportunity to revise the adjectives. It requires a mixture of comprehension and opinion on the part of the students. It is probably best done with individuals giving the responses. It could be done in tandem with **In poche parole 1D.**

▲ **Com'è Giorgio?**

■ **È spiritoso.**

▲ **Ti piace (Giorgio)?**

■ **Sì, mi piace. È simpatico.**

• *In poche parole 1D* Textbook p 23

Students could move from working in the class group to working in pairs.

• *Studiamo la lingua! A Io non sono brutto!* Workbook p 26

• *Penna in mano! C Kerry-Anne è molto simpatica!* Workbook p 20

• *Su con l'orecchio! B Com'è Adriano?* Workbook p 15, Cassette 3, tape script Teacher's Manual p 15

Carla is the girl who went up to Elena in the **fotoromanzo.** Explain to your students that they will have to listen for the adjectives the other people use to work out whether their comments are positive or negative. Notice that **birichino** is given both a positive and a negative spin in this exercise.

• *A lingua sciolta! 1 Non è vero!* Textbook p 33

Encourage your students to make the descriptions of themselves as detailed as possible. They have at least a dozen adjectives from which to choose and it might be as well to list them together and check on their meanings before you start. It would also be helpful to consolidate (**io**) **sono** and (**tu**) **sei** and to practise these forms with **non**.

Students should prepare their descriptions in writing, but should try to deliver them orally without too much reading. Inevitably, students will contradict anyone who claims to be **intelligente, bello** etc. Don't feel that these people are subverting the activity: if they understand what is being said and can counter it in correct Italian, then you are achieving the aim of the activity.

The person who correctly identifies the false adjective and is able to express this clearly should be the one to give the next description. If there are too many to make this practicable as a whole-class activity you could divide the class into groups, which you would visit and encourage.

• *Game: Chi è?*

A student writes the name of a classmate on a piece of paper and sees if the rest of the class can guess who it is. The student holds up the piece of paper and asks **Chi è questo?** The others fire questions from the body of the class: **È alto? Ha dodici anni? Abita a Epping? È intelligente? Si chiama Shaun?**

• *Rompicapi C Guarda la stella!* Workbook p 29

Solution:

1 **Giorgio è birichino.**

2 **Barbara è alta.**

3 **Luisa è antipatica.**

4 **È molto brutto.**

5 **Elena è simpatica.**

6 **È molto severa.**

7 **Adriano è forte.**

8 **È intelligente.**

The word describing Lidia: **sportiva**.

STAGE 3

- *Su con l'orecchio! C Un'intervista*
  Workbook p 15, Cassette 3, tape script
  Teacher's Manual p 15

Check that your students understand the items on the interview sheet. You might mention that Italians do have their own word for basketball, **la pallacanestro**, and go on to briefly discuss the appeal of the shorter, more American-sounding word. *Beautiful* is a popular soapie which may be known to your class as *The Bold and the Beautiful*. *Beverly Hills 90210* was recently acclaimed as the most popular series among Italian teenagers.

You may also like to talk about Madonna's Italian origin and mention that there is another well-known Madonna in Italy.

Can your students guess the meaning of **la cucina italiana**? Can they give any examples of **la pasta**?

- *A tu per tu Textbook p 21*

- *Penna in mano! D Ti piace?*
  Workbook p 20

- *A lingua sciolta! 2 Ti piace?*
  Textbook p 33

- *Datevi la mano! Textbook p 25*

Read and listen to this **fumetto**, and then move into the role-playing of the character parts. Apart from the reluctant handshake, there are some very Italian hand gestures to notice as well. Look at how Ms Gallicani is holding her hands when she first comes into the room. Show your students how to do it and have them imitate it. As well as **Che c'è?**, this gesture could be used with **Ma scusa!** The other gesture to point out is the one Ms Gallicani uses when she says **Vieni**

qui! When you show the class how to do it they may comment that it looks more like you are telling them to go away!

Incorporate these gestures into your classroom language and encourage the students to do the same. They will be more than happy to use this sort of body language when they are role-playing this and other **fumetti**. The repertoire of gestures will increase as the course progresses.

- *Su con l'orecchio! D Che classe!*
  Workbook p 16, Cassette 3, tape script
  Teacher's Manual p 16

- *Penna in mano! E Forza ragazzi!*
  Workbook p 21

STAGE 4

- *Che ore sono? Textbook p 28*

Before moving on to the times on these clocks, revise telling the time on the hour. Use the clocks from the first chapter or a clock that you have provided yourself.

The captions under the first clocks provide the pattern on which to base time-telling on the half- and quarter-hour and the in-between times. When you are asking, concentrate on the half-hours first and then come back and do the quarter-hours. Once they have mastered these, your students can tackle the in-between times.

Can you and your class work out or guess which clock is:

- a water clock in the **Pincio** gardens in Rome?
- outside the **Rinascente** department store in Rome?
- on a castle in a small town north of Rome?
- in a café in Florence?
- on a church in Rome?
- just off Lygon Street in Carlton, Melbourne?
- on the parliament building in Rome?

- *Penna in mano! F Che ore sono?*
  Workbook p 22

- *Preparatory activity*

Attention at this stage turns back to the classroom with focus on the items of school equipment the students use every day. You can prepare your class for the photo-presentation **Sempre a scuola**, by introducing the new vocabulary into your classroom language, i.e. in a communicative context.

Bring your own backpack into class: **Ecco il mio zaino! È bello, no? È nuovo. Dov'è il tuo zaino, Linda?**

Not all classes will bring bags into the room, but everyone will be able to join in when you go on: **Ecco il mio libro! Dov'è il tuo libro, Josh?** or **Ecco la mia riga! Dov'è la tua riga, Cherie?** Persist until Cherie answers: **Ecco la mia riga!**

You could then start teaching this classroom vocabulary by holding up or pointing to individual items and having the class repeat after you: **la lavagna**, **il quaderno** etc. Then see if they can name the items without your leading them.

Once the class has mastered this, reintroduce the possessive, holding aloft your pieces of equipment while your students brandish their own and repeat after you: **il mio astuccio, la mia penna** etc.

- *Sempre a scuola Textbook p 30*

Before you begin this presentation, talk about the times at which Italian students attend school. With some local variations, most start school around eight o'clock and finish at about one o'clock. Most are required to attend school on Saturday mornings as well. Introduce two new items of vocabulary: **il professore** and **la professoressa**.

Listen to and read **Sempre a scuola**. You might like to comment on:

- the blackboard with the grid lines for writing on. Most **quaderni** have lines like these.

- Italian handwriting. (What differences from their own handwriting do your students notice?)

- the task the English teacher was setting this **seconda media** class. They had to write in their **quaderni** the questions you would ask to get the answers she was writing on the board. (What do people in your class think of this exercise?)

Did your class work out who **il signor Gobbo** is?

- *Penna in mano! G Sempre a scuola, domande Workbook p 23*

- *Studiamo la lingua! B Il, la, l', lo Workbook p 26*

- *Penna in mano! H Di chi è? Workbook p 24*

- *In poche parole 2A Textbook p 32*

This is a reprise of your earlier preparatory activity and by now your students should feel quite confident about tackling it. If any of the realia are not ready at hand, students can point to items in the *Textbook* illustration.

- *Rompicapi B Brava, Bianca! Workbook p 28*

Solution:

1 **penna** 2 **zaino** 3 **diario** 4 **astuccio**
5 **quaderno** 6 **professore** 7 **tavolo** 8 **riga**
9 **libro** 10 **matita** 11 **gomma**

The place where Bianca keeps her money is in her **portafoglio**.

- *Rompicapi A No, non qui! Workbook p 27*

STAGE 5

- *Preparatory activity*

At this stage the class is ready to talk about the price of some classroom items. You can start by expressing your indignation at the cost of some of the things you have had to buy: **Questo zaino costa 40 dollari! Il mio diario costa 30 dollari.**

Prepare your students for their next reading of **Sempre a scuola** by teaching them to count by tens to a hundred. This should not be too much of a challenge since it is fairly simple and they already know **dieci**, **venti** and **cento**.

Once your students can manage this you could talk to them about Italian money, relating your discussion to the price displayed on Bianca's new **zaino**. How can they find out how many **lire** they can buy for a dollar? How hard do they think it would be to become a millionaire in Italy?

- *Sempre a scuola Textbook p 30*

Listen to and read **Sempre a scuola** a second time. This time through, you might like to comment on:

- the fashion of having English words plastered all over items such as bags and T-shirts.

- the fact that some of the older students travel to and from school on motor scooters. They are permitted to ride **motorini** up to 50 cc from the age of 14, but most can't afford them until they are older. Many parents will not allow their teenagers to ride **motorini** in the Roman traffic.
- the appearance of the students. They have no uniform, and until recently impressed visitors with the casual elegance of their dress. What do people in your class think?

- ***In poche parole 2B*** *Textbook p 32*

- ***Su con l'orecchio! F Quanto costa?*** *Workbook p 17, Cassette 3, tape script Teacher's Manual p 17*

- ***Studiamo la lingua! C Mio o mia?*** *Workbook p 27*

- ***Penna in mano! I Tu*** *Workbook p 25*

The answers that students write here will provide some raw material for their first letter to Italy which is the writing activity to follow.

- ***Rompicapi D Cruciverba*** *Workbook p 30* Solution:

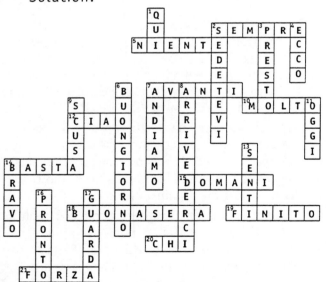

- ***Penna in mano! J Una prima lettera in Italia*** *Workbook p 25, repromaster Teacher's Manual p 18*

The idea of writing letters to the *Forza!* characters is one which could be followed throughout the rest of the course. The plan is offered as a guide only, so students should be

encouraged to think of their own things to say. (This encouragement will perhaps be more appropriate at later stages of the course, i.e. when there are lots more things to say.)

Stress to your class that this activity is the most important piece of writing they do for this chapter and that they can use it to help assess how they are progressing with the language.

Suggested assessment tasks

Listening

- ***Su con l'orecchio! C Un'intervista*** *Workbook p 15, Cassette 3, tape script Teacher's Manual p 15*

- ***Su con l'orecchio! D Che classe!*** *Workbook p 16, Cassette 3, tape script Teacher's Manual p 16*

- ***Su con l'orecchio! E Che ore sono?*** *Workbook p 17, Cassette 3, tape script Teacher's Manual p 16*

- ***Su con l'orecchio! F Quanto costa?*** *Workbook p 17, Cassette 3, tape script Teacher's Manual p 17*

Speaking

- ***In poche parole 2*** *Textbook p 32*
- ***Che ore sono?*** *Textbook p 28*
- ***A tu per tu*** *Textbook p 21*
- ***A lingua sciolta! 1 Non è vero*** *Textbook p 33*

Reading

- ***Penna in mano! B È molto intelligente!*** *Workbook p 19*

- ***Penna in mano! G Sempre a scuola*** *Workbook p 23*

Writing

Penna in mano! C Kerry-Anne è molto simpatica! *Workbook p 20*

Penna in mano! E Forza, ragazzi! *Workbook p 21*

Penna in mano! I Tu *Workbook p 25*

Penna in mano! J Una prima lettera in Italia *Workbook p 25, repromaster Teacher's Manual p 18*

Capitolo 2

Su con l'orecchio!
Tape scripts

A Chi è?

La signora Gallicani and another of Angela's teachers are watching from a window as the students arrive at school. Under each picture write a number to show who they are talking about and then the word they use to describe them.

1 – Come si chiama lui?
 – Chi? Lui?
 – No, lui.
 – Ah, si chiama Adriano.
 – Adriano?
 – Sì, è nuovo.

2 – Ah, ecco Antonella!
 – Dove?
 – Guarda!
 – Ah, sì. Mi piace Antonella. È brava.

3 – Chi è questa?
 – Si chiama Angela.
 – È nuova?
 – No, non è nuova.
 – È bella.
 – Sì, è molto bella.

4 – Ed ecco Giorgio!
 – Senti, com'è Giorgio?
 – Com'è Giorgio? È birichino, molto birichino. Ma mi piace.

5 – Come si chiama lei?
 – Chi?
 – Lei.
 – Ah, si chiama Elena.
 – Mm, è alta. È sportiva?
 – No, non è sportiva.

6 – Ecco Barbara.
 – Barbara? Dove?
 – Eccola! Guarda!
 – Ah, lei è la famosa Barbara. Com'è?
 – È simpatica. Mi piace molto.

B Com'è Adriano?

Elena's friend Carla can't stop talking about the new boy Adriano and she is keen to know what others think about him. Listen to what the others say and work out whether they have something good (positive) or something bad (negative) to say. Place a tick in the appropriate column.

1 – Ti piace il nuovo ragazzo?
 – Chi, Adriano?
 – Adriano, sì.
 – Sì, mi piace. È simpatico.

2 – Ecco Adriano. È nuovo. Ti piace?
 – Boh, è brutto.

3 – Adriano non è molto alto.
 – No, ma è forte. È molto sportivo.

4 – Com'è Adriano?
 – È intelligente. È molto bravo in italiano e storia.

5 – Scusa, dov'è Adriano?
 – Adriano? Il nuovo? Che antipatico!

6 – Adriano è il mio amico.
 – Sei fortunata! Lui è molto bello.

7 – Conosci Adriano?
 – Sì, è birichino.
 – Non ti piace, allora?
 – Sì, mi piace. È birichino. È bravo.

8 – Ecco Adriano.
 – Sì, Adriano. Che brutto! Che antipatico!
 – È il mio amico!!!
 – Oh, mi dispiace!

C Un'intervista

Antonella is interviewing Giorgio for the class newspaper. Help her out by recording his likes and dislikes on the interview sheet she has prepared. Place a tick in the appropriate column.

 – Senti, Giorgio, ti piace la scuola?
 – La scuola? Be', insomma...
 – La scuola, Giorgio. Ti piace o no?
 – No, non mi piace.
 – Va bene. Ti piace l'italiano?

– L'italiano, sì, mi piace. Mi piace molto.

– E la matematica?

– Sì, mi piace la matematica.

– Non ti piace la scuola, ma ti piace l'italiano e la matematica. Mamma mia! Senti, Giorgio, ti piace lo sport?

– Ma sì. Io sono molto sportivo. Sono alto, sono forte, sono...

– Va bene, va bene. Il tennis? Ti piace?

– Sì.

– E il basket?

– Sì, mi piace. Sono molto bravo in...

– Grazie, Giorgio! Ti piace la televisione?

– Sì, molto.

– Ti piace *Beautiful*?

– *Beautiful*?! Che schifo!!

– E *Beverly Hills*, ti piace?

– Sì, mi piace.

– Ti piace la musica, Giorgio?

– Mmm, sì...sì.

– Midnight Oil?

– Come?

– Ti piace Midnight Oil?

– No. È musica classica?

– Madonna!

– Come?

– Madonna. Ti piace Madonna?

– Sì, mi piace molto. Madonna è bella, è brava, è intelligente...

– Sì, Giorgio, grazie, Giorgio. E finalmente, ti piace la cucina italiana?

– No, non mi piace.

– Ti piace la pizza?

– Sì, mi piace la pizza, ma la pizza è americana, no?

– E la pasta?

– Sì, mi piace la pasta...spaghetti, lasagne...

– Uffa!

D Che classe!

La signora Gallicani has her hands full with Giorgio, Luisa and the rest of the class. In fact, her hands often help her make her meaning clear. Write the appropriate number under these pictures to show that you have understood what she is saying.

1 – Presto! Vieni qui! Subito!

2 – Ma scusa! Che c'è?!

3 – Silenzio! Sta zitta!

4 – Andiamo, ragazzi! Forza! Avanti!

5 – Ma guarda! Guarda!

6 – Tu, siediti qui. E tu, siediti qui!

7 – Ciao, bella! Come stai?

8 – Uffa!

E Che ore sono?

Listen for the time and then write it in on these digital clocks.

1 – Scusa, che ore sono?
   – Guarda! Sono le dieci e mezzo.

2 – Andiamo, ragazzi! Presto, sono le otto e un quarto.

3 – Sei pronta, Barbara?
   – No, non sono pronta, mamma.
   – Presto, cara, sono le nove meno un quarto.

4 – Sono in ritardo?
   – No, non sei in ritardo. È l'una e mezzo.
   – L'una e mezzo precise?
   – Sì, precise. Allora, come stai oggi?

5 – Buonasera. Questa è la radio 903.4 a Roma. Sono le cinque meno un quarto. Adesso un po' di musica di...Madonna!

6 – Mamma mia! La lezione è finita?!
   – Sì, signora. Sono le undici e venticinque.
   – Va bene. Arrivederci, ragazzi.
   – Arrivederci, signora.
   – Arrivederci.

7 – Sono le nove e quaranta.
   – No, sono le dieci meno venti.
   – No, sono le nove e quaranta.
   – No, sono le dieci meno venti.
   – No, sono le nove e quaranta.
   – No, sono le...

8 – Mi dispiace, sono in ritardo.
   – No, non sei in ritardo. Sono le otto meno cinque. Abbiamo cinque minuti.

9 – Mamma mia, guarda l'ora!
 – Che ore sono?
 – Sono le sette e...e diciotto.
 – Presto, andiamo!

10 – Che ore sono, per favore?
 – Le quattro e quattro.
 – Come, le quattro e un quarto?
 – No, le quattro e quattro.
 – Grazie.
 – Prego.

F Quanto costa?

You have a holiday job at the local school supplier and today there is a one-day, back-to-school sale. Mark in the sale prices of the different items as the manager tells you what they are.

1 – Sei pronto? Allora, l'astuccio: 7000 lire.

2 – Il quaderno costa 1000 lire. Sì, solo 1000 lire.

3 – La gomma, mmm...quanto costa la gomma oggi? Ah sì, 500 lire.

4 – La matita, oggi, e solo oggi, 200 lire.

5 – Il portafoglio – e bello, no? Ti piace? Il portafoglio costa 10 000 lire.

6 – Lo zaino non costa 30 000 lire, no. Oggi, solo 20 000 lire.

7 – La riga: 1500 lire. Capito? 1500 lire.

8 – Il libro: 15 000 lire.

9 – E questa bella penna, quanto costa? 1000 lire? No. 900 lire? No. Oggi, solo 800 lire.

10 – E finalmente, il diario. Oggi il diario costa 5000 lire.

Caro Scarno,

Mi chiamo Travis, ho dodici anni e abito a Mill Park. Mill Park è a Melbourne, in Australia.

La mia scuola si chiama Northern Secondary College. La mia classe è Year 7D.

Io sono piccolo, ma sono molto sportivo. Sono bravo in tennis e in basket.
Mi piace la NBA. Michael Jordan è alto e forte e molto veloce.

Non sono molto intelligente, ma mi piace la scuola. Non sono molto bravo in italiano, ma mi piace. La mia professoressa d'italiano si chiama Ms Nocera.
È severa ma è molto simpatica.

Ti piace la musica, Scarno? Ti piace Alanis Morrissette? È bella, no? Ti piace la televisione? Mi piace Home and Away e mi piace I Simpsons. Bart Simpson è molto birichino.

Ti piace la scuola, Scarno? Ti piace l'inglese? Com'è la signora Gallicani?
È molto severa? Com'è Roma? È bella?

Ciao, Scarno.

Il tuo amico,
Travis Stevens

Forza! uno student progress sheet

In the **io** column, give yourself a tick for each thing that you know how to do in Italian. Then ask a friend to check you and mark the **amico/a** column. Keep the last column free for when your teacher has time to hear how you are progressing.

Nome _____ **Classe** _____

Capitolo 2	io	amico/a	
Ask people if they like something			
Say that you like something			
Say you don't like something			
Ask what someone is like			
Ask people if they like someone			
Say that you like someone			
Say you don't like someone			
Describe yourself			
Describe someone else			
Tell the time at any time			
Say what's in your school bag			
Say what's in your pencil case			
Ask where something is			
Say whose it is			
Say that something is yours			
Count by 10s to 100			
Ask how much something costs			
Say how much something costs			
Tell someone to hurry			
Tell someone to listen			
Tell someone to be quiet			
Tell someone to come here			
Tell someone that's enough			

Suggested procedure

STAGE 1

• *Preparatory activity 1*

To help establish one of the main themes for the chapter, you could bring into class some of your own family photos and introduce the people in them to your students: **Questa è la mia famiglia. Questo è mio padre. Questa è mia madre. Questa è mia sorella, Jane. È bella, no? È molto simpatica. Questo è mio fratello, Paul. Lui è un po' matto.** (Use an appropriate gesture to help them understand. Suggest to the students that they ask an Italian friend about the hand gestures they can use.) **E questo è il mio piccolo fratello, Stephen. Ho una sorella e due fratelli.**

(Note: In *Sempre Avanti*, pages 36–7, some of the more common hand gestures are illustrated.)

To further prepare your class for the **fotoromanzo**, it might be a good idea to write the key items of vocabulary on the board. Introduce the plural forms the class needs at the moment: **fratello–fratelli, sorella–sorelle.**

• *A casa con i Ferraro* Textbook p 37

Listen to and read the **fotoromanzo**. Ask your students to concentrate on who's who in the Ferraro family and what they are like. They should try not to be put off by other new language.

• *Domande 1* Textbook p 40

Do these questions orally first. Do not insist on answers in complete sentences, allowing students to respond as naturally as possible. For example, in response to the question **Quanti fratelli ha Lucio?**, the response **Uno** is perfectly acceptable.

• *Penna in mano! A Domande 1* Workbook p 34

Before they begin their written answers in the *Workbook*, explain to your students that this is a good chance to practise writing full Italian sentences. It would be helpful to give them an example of a full-sentence response to the three different types of questions here: **Quanti/e? Come si chiama? Com'è?**

• *Studiamo la lingua! A Il, la, l', lo* Workbook p 44

• *Preparatory activity 2*

Move on to asking students about their own families: **Io ho due fratelli. E tu? Quanti fratelli hai? Ah, non hai fratelli! Quante sorelle hai? Come si chiama tuo fratello? Com'è tua sorella? Ti piace?**

• *A tu per tu* Textbook p 41

Use this oral exercise to help students structure the language they are using about their families. Note that they may be required to say **mi piacciono** at the conclusion of this conversation. For the time being, it would be enough to explain that you say **mi piace** if you are talking about one sister, **mi piacciono** if you are talking about more than one.

• *Su con l'orecchio! A Quanti fratelli e sorelle hai?* Workbook p 31, Cassette 3, tape script Teacher's Manual p 26

First, do this listening exercise as it is set out, pausing and repeating the tape as is appropriate for your class. Once you have corrected the students' answers, you could go through the tape again and listen for the additional information and comments that fill out these conversations. Here are some extra questions you could use:

1 What do they say about the size of this family?

2 And what about this family? What do they say about the house?

3 What is this person's family situation? Are they happy with it?

4 What comment is made about the size of this family?

5 Is this person happy with their family situation?

6 Apart from the number of people in it, do we learn about this person's family situation?

• *A lingua sciolta! 1 La mia famiglia* Textbook p 41

• *Studiamo la lingua! B Un, una, un', uno* Workbook p 44

STAGE 2

• *Preparatory activity*

At the risk of being predictable in your teaching strategies, why not bring in a photo of your house or flat? Your class will appreciate this extra light shed on your private life: **Questa è la mia casa. Non è molto grande, ma mi piace. Ha tre camere da letto.**

You could then move to the board and model for your class the **A lingua sciolta!** activity they will be doing later. Sketch a floor plan and indicate the various rooms around your place: **Questo è il salotto. Guardo la televisione qui. Ecco il bagno. La cucina è qui. E qui ho un piccolo giardino.**

There is no mention of **il giardino** in this chapter of the *Textbook* since the Ferraros live in an apartment. You will need to add **il giardino** to the vocabulary for the time being. It might be necessary to restrict the growth of this house vocabulary or your list could reach unmanageable proportions as students ask about family rooms, billiard rooms, sun rooms, pools, spas etc.

It may be opportune to point out that when Italians move to other countries they make up words for things they did not have in Italy, such as **la fenza** and **la becciarda**. At the same time it is important to avoid generalisations such as 'Italians live in flats so they don't have yards'.

• *A casa con i Ferraro* Textbook p 37

The focus for this reading is on the flat where Francesco lives with his family.

The Ferraros have two of the balconies on the second floor. One is off **il salotto** while Francesco's bedroom opens onto the other. As do many Italian families, the Ferraros have an apartment in a busy part of town. You can see **il bar** above which they live and there will be other glimpses of various shops along the street below them. You could explain briefly what **un bar** is in Italy.

You could point out that as is the case for apartment-dwellers everywhere, **il balcone** has an important role to play as somewhere to put pot-plants and dry the washing (see frame 8).

• *Domande 2* Textbook p 42

Once again, do these questions orally first,

allowing students to respond as naturally as possible. When you follow this up with written answers in the *Workbook* ask them to practise writing full Italian sentences.

• *Penna in mano! B Domande 2* *Workbook p 35*

Revise the question words your class is already familiar with: **Quanti/e?** and **Com'è?** Then make sure they understand **Dove?** You could give them an example of a full-sentence response to a **Dove?** question: **La famiglia Ferraro abita a Roma.**

• *Su con l'orecchio! B Dove sono?* *Workbook p 31, Cassette 3, tape script Teacher's Manual p 26*

First, do this listening exercise as it is set out, pausing and repeating the tape as is appropriate for your class. As you correct their answers, ask your students to specify the language or other clues that helped them identify the room in question.

You could then go through the tape again and listen for extra information and comments. See if your class can tell you:

1 What Maura says that shows she can be a bit sarcastic.
2 What Antonio is watching on TV and what Maura thinks of it.
3 Why Antonio is a bit cross with Francesco and what excuse Francesco gives.
4 What Francesco is doing, what he thinks of it, where Lucio is when they are talking and what he decides to do next.
5 What the family is having for dinner.
6 Why Lucio calls his brother **spiritoso**. (Your class will meet this word soon in the **fumetto** but they might be able to guess its meaning from the context here.)

• *In poche parole 2A* Textbook p 47

• *In poche parole 2B* Textbook p 47

You could draw attention to **Dov'è?**, explaining that what looks and sounds like one word is actually formed from two.

• *Penna in mano! C Dove sono?* *Workbook p 36*

• *Studiamo la lingua! C I plurali* *Workbook p 44*

- *A lingua sciolta! 2 La mia casa*
  Textbook p 42

STAGE 3

• *A casa con i Ferraro* Textbook p 37

The emphasis in this final reading of the **fotoromanzo** is on what the different members of the family are doing. This will, of course, involve introducing your students to the wonders of Italian verbs. In this chapter the repertoire has been restricted to half a dozen **-are** verbs which they will practise in a number of different settings.

The communicative demands of this chapter have also led to some more work on **essere** as well as the introduction of **fare** and **avere**. It is vital that you and your students take seriously the note in the **Studiamo la lingua!** section: 'you will have many opportunities to learn more about and to practise Italian verbs.' It is not essential for your students to achieve complete mastery of the material presented here before they can proceed with the course.

• *Domande 3* Textbook p 44

In most cases your students can answer these questions by reading the appropriate sections of the text. They will notice that this does not work when they are talking about Francesco. Can they work out why? A similar situation arises with question 7.

- • *Penna in mano! D A casa con i Ferraro: Domande 3* Workbook p 47

- • *Rompicapi A A casa con i Ferraro* Workbook p 47
  Solution: See top of following column for the word puzzle solution.

- • *Su con l'orecchio! C Che cosa fai?* Workbook p 32, Cassette 3, tape script Teacher's Manual p 27

This exercise will prepare your students for the following **In poche parole** exercises by making clear what each character is doing. Someone may notice that Maura and Barbara are already eating spaghetti while Dario is supposed to be cooking it. What has obviously happened is that Dario's first batch was such a hit that he has had to make some more! Who did Giorgio not know before this get-together?

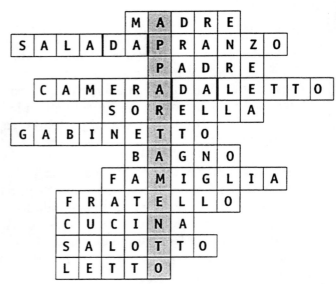

(Rompicapi A *Workbook p 47*, Solution)

• *In poche parole 2C* Textbook p 47

In this exercise your students will be dealing with the third person singular only so that they can concentrate on the meanings of these new verbs.

You might decide to leave Luisa and Lidia out of contention for the time being. **Aspettare** meaning 'to wait *for*' may be a little difficult at this stage, and what Lidia is doing in the toilet is a bit tricky to talk about.

- • *In poche parole 2D* Textbook p 47

- • *Penna in mano! E Che cosa fanno?* Workbook p 38

- • *Studiamo la lingua! D Che buono!* Workbook p 44

- • *Studiamo la lingua! E Che forte!* Workbook p 45

- • *Studiamo la lingua! F Al plurale!* Workbook p 45

STAGE 4

• *Preparatory activity*

Prepare your class for the **fumetto** to follow with some brief conversations about helping around the house: **Voi aiutate la mamma a casa/in cucina? Tuo padre prepara la cena? Qualche volta? Sempre? Tu fai i piatti? Ah, sei un bravo ragazzo! Mamma mia, sei molto pigra!**

This introductory activity lets students hear and start to use different persons of **-are** verbs such as **aiutare** and **preparare**. If you decide at this stage to give a thorough explanation of how these verbs work, you could use **abitare** as your model. Your students are already familiar with **io abito**, **tu abiti** and **lui/lei abita**. They should be ready for an initial exposure to the plural forms of this verb.

In terms of the more formal learning of verbs, concentrate on the regular **-are** verbs. The communicative needs of this chapter mean that forms of **fare**, **essere** and **avere** occur quite frequently, but the exercises and activities make clear that there is not the same focus on the formal learning of these verbs. They are set out in the grammar section of this chapter for reference only, and will be followed up as the course progresses.

• *La squadra Ferraro* Textbook p 50

This **fumetto** introduces the theme of family as a team and touches on the issue of gender roles in the division of household labour. You could reflect with your class on the predicament of Maura, living in a house with three males. In the **fotoromanzo** Antonio takes an active role in preparing the dinner and is involved with his children. In the **fumetto** he reverts to behaviour that has been more readily associated with Italian men. He is doing his best to be a sensitive new-age male but is prone to the occasional soccer-induced lapse. Maura could capitulate and adopt the role of a more traditional Italian **mamma**, spoiling both her husband and her sons. She opts instead to do her bit for **la liberazione della donna**.

Ask the students how we know that, when Maura says **Sono pigri!**, in this case, **sono** doesn't mean 'I am'.

• *Non dire stupidaggini!*
  Textbook p 52

This is obviously just a more sophisticated form of **Vero o falso?** exercise. Before you start it, give the class plenty of vigorous practice at exclaiming indignantly **Non dire stupidaggini!** Once they have the hang of it, you could make up a whole series of **stupidaggini** to let them react to:

1 **Io sono molto timido.**
2 **Io sono antipatica.**
3 **Io sono molto severa.**
4 **Io non sono molto intelligente.**
5 **Ho diciannove anni.**

The next step would be for the students to go on to correct you: **Tu non sei timido**. And then, even: **Tu sei spiritoso!** (We're still happy for them to use the familiar form of address with us, aren't we?) **Non dire stupidaggini!** could well become an oft-repeated expression around your classroom.

• *Penna in mano! G Non scrivere stupidaggini!* Workbook p 40

• *Su con l'orecchio! D Come sono?* Workbook p 32, Cassette 3, tape script Teacher's Manual p 27

• *Rompicapi B Sei una brava spia?* Workbook p 48

Solution: 1 **il pane** 2 **le penne** 3 **la torta** 4 **la pasta** 5 **gli spaghetti** 6 **le tagliatelle** 7 **le lasagne** 8 **il sugo** 9 **il dolce** 10 **i ravioli** 11 **la verdura** 12 **le farfalle** 13 **buon appetito**

• *In poche parole 1A* Textbook p 45

This exercise gives some thorough oral practice of an **-are** verb. The fact that the names of the different sports are (mostly) borrowed from English allows students to concentrate on the forms that **giocare** takes according to person and number.

In order to practise the full range of present-tense forms, your students will be required to speak *to* and *for* the characters, as well as about them. In the first instance, have the class respond as a whole if you think they need to practise in this way, and then move on to having individuals or pairs respond for the characters.

The one form that is not practised here is the third person singular; it has already been thoroughly practised in previous oral exercises. You could revise this form as you familiarise your students with the illustration: **Chi gioca a ping-pong? Che cosa fa Scarno? Francesco gioca a tennis?**

Why would it be that Italian has a word of its own for soccer, yet borrows words such as 'baseball' from English?

- **Penna in mano! F Viva lo sport!** *Workbook p 39*

Whereas you would not have insisted on complete sentences in your oral preparation for **In poche parole 1A**, this is a good opportunity for the class to practise writing sentences in full.

- **In poche parole 1B** *Textbook p 45*

There is no need to fence off sections A, B, and C of this exercise as separate entities. Once you judge your class to be ready for it, you can break down the mechanical and repetitive nature of the drill by ranging across the different sections, mixing and matching the various cues and responses.

- **In poche parole 1C** *Textbook p 45*

You can expect a number of students to have trouble pronouncing **giocano**. It may be helpful to point out that, for pronunciation as well as written purposes, you simply add **-no** to the singular form: **gioca-giocano**. You could pursue this point by practising with **aiuta-no**, **mangia-no**, **parla-no**, **prepara-no** and **taglia-no**.

- **Studiamo la lingua! G Parlare di 'are'** *Workbook p 45*

- **Studiamo la lingua! H Quanti verbi!** *Workbook p 46*

STAGE 5

- **La squadra Ferraro** *Textbook p 50*

Once they have listened to and read this **fumetto** again, your students will be ready to role-play the different character parts. You could draw attention to Maura's wishing the boys **Buon lavoro!** Your class has already seen and heard **Buon appetito!** in this chapter and might be interested to know that Italians do usually wish one another well with whatever activity they are about to tackle, whether this be a walk, a holiday, a trip – or whatever! You could give some examples or ask students to be on the look-out for similar **auguri** as they occur during the course. **Buon lavoro!** is one that would often be appropriate in your classroom.

- **In poche parole 3A** *Textbook p 53*

The illustration includes some of the most popular pasta shapes, but is obviously not meant to be exhaustive. You could extend the exploration of this topic in a number of ways but you may prefer to leave some details for treatment at a later date. If you have not already done so, you could explain the expression **al dente** at this point. Do you subscribe to the 'throw-it-against-the wall-to see-if-it-sticks' theory?

Although there is mention of **il sugo** in the **fotoromanzo** and **fumetto**, specific examples are not given until later in the course when there is an opportunity for your students to cook a pasta dish.

There is obviously no 'right' answer to the question here; just choose any of the pasta dishes illustrated. You could link exercises A and B so that there is more of a continuing conversation.

- **In poche parole 3B** *Textbook p 53*

- **Penna in mano! H Mi piace la pasta** *Workbook p 41*

- **In poche parole 3C** *Textbook p 53*

This little dialogue has a different setting from A and B: you could be asking a waiter in a restaurant before you make your choice, or speaking to someone who is eating the pasta you are inquiring about.

Your students will notice that words like **spaghetti** and **lasagne** are plural words, whereas we tend to think of them as singular nouns in English. They may also understand why some of them have the names they do. The butterfly over the **farfalle** should be a help, they could make an educated guess at **penne**, they know a word from this chapter that makes up the first part of **tagliatelle** and will be interested to know that **lo spago** means 'string'. Someone in the class might know that **tagliatelle** are also called **fettuccine**.

- **Su con l'orecchio! E Che cosa mangiamo?** *Workbook p 33, Cassette 3, tape script Teacher's Manual p 28*

Once the basic exercise has been completed and corrected, you could follow up with some further questions to see if your students have understood other elements of these brief conversations:

1. Why did dad change his plans for the evening's menu?

2. Why was mum a bit cross with her daughter?

3. a Why did they have to wait for the spaghetti?

   b How long did they have to wait?

   c What did they do while they waited?

4. a What was the invitation?

   b Why was it not accepted?

5. Why does the daughter say that mum is **spiritosa**?

6. a Why is dad a bit cross with his son?

   b What sort of vegies are they having?

- *Su con l'orecchio! F Test*
  Workbook p 33, Cassette 3, tape script Teacher's Manual p 29

This listening exercise will provide a helpful model for the **Test** your students are about to perform as an oral activity in the **A lingua sciolta!** style. Before tackling this listening exercise in the *Workbook*, familiarise them with the activity as outlined on page 54 of the *Textbook*.

You could tell them that this sort of 'test' is very common in Italian magazines and is a *very* reliable way of finding out all sorts of things about yourself. This one needs to be taken just as seriously!

- *Penna in mano! I Fai il bravo/la brava? Workbook p 42*

Answering a question in a full sentence with 'never' presents the extra grammatical difficulty of the double negative **non...mai**. There is no need to make a big issue of it; just tell the class if they use **mai** they have to write **non** in front of the verb.

- *Test Textbook p 54, repromaster Teacher's Manual p 30*

- *Penna in mano! J Che cosa dire? Workbook p 43*

- *Studiamo la lingua! I Verbi irregolari I Workbook p 46*

- *Studiamo la lingua! J Verbi irregolari II Workbook p 46*

- *Rompicapi C Cruciverba*
  Workbook p 49

Solution:

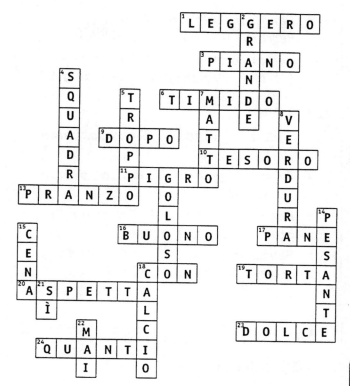

- *Penna in mano! K Una seconda lettera in Italia Workbook p 43, repromaster Teacher's Manual p 31*

Suggested assessment tasks

Listening

- *Su con l'orecchio! A Quanti fratelli e sorelle hai? Workbook p 31, Cassette 3, tape script Teacher's Manual p 26*

- *Su con l'orecchio! F Test*
  Workbook p 33, Cassette 3, tape script Teacher's Manual p 29

- *Su con l'orecchio! D Come sono?*
  Workbook p 32, Cassette 3, tape script Teacher's Manual p 27

Speaking

- *In poche parole 2B and D*
  Textbook p 47

- *A tu per tu Textbook p 41*

- *A lingua sciolta! 2 La mia casa*
  Textbook p 42

- **Test** *Textbook p 54, repromaster Teacher's Manual p 30*

Reading

- **Penna in mano! A A casa con i Ferraro: Domande 1** *Workbook p 34*
- **Penna in mano! D A casa con i Ferraro: Domande 3** *Workbook p 37*

Writing

- **Penna in mano! E Che cosa fanno!** *Workbook p 38*
- **Penna in mano! F Viva lo sport!** *Workbook p 39*
- **Penna in mano! I Fai il bravo/la brava?** *Workbook p 42*
- **Penna in mano! K Una seconda lettera in Italia** *Workbook p 43, repromaster Teacher's Manual p 31*

Su con l'orecchio!
Tape scripts

A Quanti fratelli e sorelle hai?

Listen as these people respond to a survey about the size of their families. Highlight the correct number of brothers and sisters for each person.

1 – Ciao!
  – Ciao!
  – Scusa, quanti fratelli hai?
  – Ho un fratello.
  – Allora, fratelli, uno. E sorelle? Hai sorelle?
  – No, non ho sorelle.
  – Hai una famiglia piccola.
  – Mmm, piccola, sì. Non è grande.
  – Grazie.
  – Prego.

2 – Scusa, quanti fratelli e sorelle hai?
  – Io?
  – Sì, tu. Hai fratelli e sorelle?
  – Sì, ho tre fratelli e cinque sorelle!
  – Tre fratelli e cinque sorelle!!! Mamma mia, che famiglia!
  – È grande, no?
  – Sì, è molto grande.

  – Com'è la tua casa?
  – Grande.

3 – Senti, quanti fratelli hai?
  – Non ho fratelli.
  – Va bene. E quante sorelle hai?
  – Non ho sorelle.
  – Sei solo, allora.
  – No, abito con mio padre e mia madre.
  – E ti piace così?
  – Sì, mi piace.

4 – Hai una famiglia grande o piccola?
  – Be' non so. Ho una sorella...
  – Una sorella, sì...
  – ...e un fratello.
  – Una sorella, un fratello. Una famiglia media, insomma.
  – È media? Va bene, è media.

5 – Scusa, ho delle domande sulla famiglia, fratelli, sorelle...
  – Domande? Sì, va bene. Cosa vuoi sapere?
  – Allora, quanti fratelli hai?
  – Ho tre fratelli.
  – E sorelle?
  – Sorelle, sì.
  – Quante?
  – Due.
  – Siete una grande famiglia, allora. Ti piace?
  – Qualche volta sì, qualche volta no.
  – Ho capito. Grazie.
  – Prego. Arrivederci.

6 – Io ho una sorella.
  – Mmm. Com'è questa sorella? Ti piace?
  – Mi piace, sì, è simpatica, ma lei abita con mio padre. Io abito con mia madre.
  – Ho capito. Hai fratelli?
  – No, non ho fratelli.
  – Grazie. Arrivederci.
  – Ciao!

B Dove sono?

Listen to these conversations and work out where the different people are. Use a highlighter to show you have understood.

1 – Mamma mia, questi piatti! Francesco, mi aiuti con i piatti?
  – Sì, mamma.
  – Vieni qui, subito!
  – Sì, mamma. Dove sei?
  – Facciamo i piatti in camera da letto? Macchè! Sono in cucina!

2 – Che cosa guardi, tesoro?
  – È il basket. L'Italia e il Messico. È fantastico. Vieni, siediti qui, tesoro.
  – Sempre lo sport! No, grazie. Io vado a letto. Buona notte.
  – Buona notte.

3 – Aspetta, Francesco, sei goloso!
  – Mi dispiace, papà, ma mi piacciono questi spaghetti. Sono molto buoni!
  – Allora, buon appetito!
  – Buon appetito!

4 – Uffa, non mi piacciono questi compiti! Non mi piace inglese.
  – Forza, Francesco! Tu parli inglese molto bene.
  – Sta zitto! E tu, non hai compiti?
  – No.
  – Ma su, Lucio, è il mio letto.
  – E va bene. Io vado a guardare la televisione.

5 – Gli spaghetti sono pronti, tesoro?
  – Un momento. Sì, sono al dente!
  – Bene! Questo sugo è pronto. Andiamo in sala da pranzo!
  – Sì, andiamo! Francesco, Lucio, a tavola! Il pranzo è pronto.

6 – Presto, Lucio.
  – Aspetta, aspetta!
  – Ma presto! Non hai finito? Che cosa fai? Giochi a Game Boy?
  – Spiritoso. Un momento! Ecco! Ho finito.
  – Finalmente!

C Che cosa fai?

Giorgio wasn't invited to the big get-together and is feeling very left out of things. Listen as he goes around the apartment, asking people what they are doing. Write a number next to each person to show that you know in what order they speak with him.

1 – Buongiorno, signor Ferraro. Ah, calcio.
  – Ah, ciao, Giorgio. Sì, mi piace il calcio. La mia squadra gioca oggi. Forza Roma!

2 – Scusa, tu chi sei?
  – Buongiorno, Giorgio. Io sono Scarno.
  – Va bene, Scarno, che cosa fai qui?
  – Taglio la torta. Mmm, è molto buona!

3 – E chi è questo?
  – Questo è il mio amico Roberto.
  – Ciao, Roberto. Ma tu, che cosa fai qui?
  – Aiuto Scarno con la torta. Lui taglia e io mangio.
  – Che bravo!

4 – Ciao, Dario. Cosa fai?
  – Preparo gli spaghetti. Un momento...aah sì, sono al dente!

5 – E tu aiuti Dario con gli spaghetti? Che brava!
  – Io faccio sempre la brava. Gli spaghetti sono al dente, Dario.

6 – Ah, buon appetito, signora!
  – Grazie, Giorgio. Questi spaghetti sono molto buoni. Ti piacciono, Barbara?
  – Sì, questo sugo è molto buono.

7 – Ma scusate, che cosa fate?
  – Noi? Facciamo i compiti.
  – Spiritoso. Va bene, giocate a Game Boy. Lui, chi è?
  – È mio fratello Lucio. Ecco, Lucio, tocca a te.

8 – Presto, Lidia! Lidiaaa! Presto!
  – Ah, Luisa, anche tu sei qui! Sta zitta! Che cosa fai?
  – Aspetto Lidia, è in gabinetto. Presto, Lidiaaa!

D Come sono?

Scarno is doing some interviews to find out more about how young people live these days. Choose the word from the list below that you think best describes the people he talks to. Write the word next to the appropriate number.

pesante matto timido pigro goloso spiritoso forte intelligente

1 – Ma tu non parli!
  – No, non parlo molto.
  – Non parli con gli amici?
  – Sì, parlo con gli amici.
  – Va bene. Facciamo una fotografia?
  – No, grazie. Non mi piacciono le fotografie.
  – Va bene. Ciao, allora.
  – Ciao.

2 – Fai i compiti?
  – No, non mi piacciono i compiti.
  – Fai il tuo letto?
  – No, papà fa il mio letto.
  – Fai i piatti dopo cena?
  – No, mio fratello fa i piatti.
  – E tu non aiuti.
  – No, io guardo la televisione.
  – Tuo fratello fa i piatti e tu guardi la televisione?!
  – Non sempre.
  – Ah, non sempre. Allora, qualche volta...
  – Qualche volta gioco con il Game Boy.
  – Uffa!

3 – Che cosa mangi, gli spaghetti o i ravioli?
  – Mangio gli spaghetti e i ravioli.
  – Spaghetti e ravioli!
  – Sì, e le lasagne e le tagliatelle.
  – Mamma mia, che appetito! E mangi un dolce?
  – Sì, mangio questa torta.
  – Non tagli la torta? È molto grande!
  – Non dire stupidaggini! Ah, mmm, molto buona!

4 – Ma guardi la televisione in bagno?!
  – Sì, papà è in gabinetto oggi.
  – Come? E dov'è il tuo letto? In sala da pranzo?
  – Non dire stupidaggini! Il mio letto è in cucina.
  – E fai i piatti in salotto?
  – Sì! Anche tu?
  – Uffa!

5 – Che cosa fai?
  – La matematica. Ecco, è finito!
  – Mamma mia, sei molto veloce.
  – Non molto, ma mi piace la matematica.

– E adesso che cosa fai? Questo libro non è in italiano.
– No, è indonesiano.
– Indonesiano! Parli indonesiano?
– Sì. Parlo inglese, italiano e indonesiano.
– Che bravo!

E Che cosa mangiamo?

In houses and apartments all over Rome, people are having pasta for dinner tonight. Highlight the type each family has decided on.

1 – Che cosa mangiamo a cena stasera?
  – Mangiamo spaghetti.
  – Ma non mi piacciono gli spaghetti, papà.
  – Va bene, abbiamo anche tagliatelle.
  – Bene, mi piacciono le tagliatelle.
  – Boh, mangiamo tagliatelle, allora.

2 – Ah, farfalle! Fantastico!
  – Piano, mangia piano! Mamma mia, sei golosa!
  – Mi dispiace, mamma, ma lo sai che mi piacciono le farfalle.

3 – Gli spaghetti sono al dente?
  – Mmm, no, ancora trenta secondi.
  – Va bene. Ti piace questo sugo?
  – Mmm, sì, è molto buono.
  – Come sono gli spaghetti adesso?
  – Un momento! Sì, sono pronti! Sono al dente!

4 – Come sono le lasagne?
  – Molto buone! Prego, siediti, mangia un po'.
  – No, grazie, non mi piacciono le lasagne.

5 – Scusa, mamma, hai una penna?
  – Ho cento penne qui.
  – Come? Ah, spiritosa! Mangiamo penne a cena, allora?
  – Sì, e sono pronte adesso. Tu sei pronta?

6 – Buon appetito!
  – Buon appetito!
  – Passa i ravioli, per favore.
  – Ecco i ravioli, e mangia anche un po' di verdura stasera!
  – Sì, papà, ma non mi piace la verdura.
  – Non dire stupidaggini! Queste zucchine sono molto buone!

F Test

Listen to this boy performing the **Sei un bravo ragazzo?** test. Score 5 points for each time he answers **sempre**, 3 for **qualche volta** and 1 point for **mai**. Add up the points at the end to see if he is **un angelo**, **un bravissimo ragazzo**, **un bravo ragazzo** or **un diavolo**.

1 – Allora, sei pronto per queste domande?
 – Sì, avanti! Sono pronto.
 – Aiuti tuo padre o tua madre a casa?
 – Aiuto mia madre in giardino.
 – Che cosa fai?
 – Taglio l'erba.
 – Sempre?
 – Sì, sempre.
 – Bravo! Cinque punti.

2 – Fai il tuo letto?
 – Mmm, qualche volta.
 – Non sempre?
 – No, qualche volta. Qualche volta.
 – Va bene, va bene.

3 – Allora, fai la spesa qualche volta?
 – Chi, io?
 – Sì, tu!
 – No, mio padre fa la spesa.
 – E tu, mai?
 – Mai!

4 – Prepari la cena?
 – No, mai...Un momento, sì, qualche volta.
 – Ah, sì, che cosa fai?
 – Telefono per la pizza.
 – Telefoni per la pizza...ma...Va bene, 3 punti.
 – Grazie.

5 – Fai i piatti dopo cena?
 – No, faccio i compiti dopo cena.
 – Chi fa i piatti?
 – Mia sorella.
 – E tua sorella non ha compiti?
 – Sì, ma, insomma...
 – E tu non fai mai i piatti. Sei pigro!

6 – Mangi la verdura?
 – Qualche volta, ma non mi piace.
 – Non ti piacciono le zucchine? Sono deliziose!
 – Le zucchine? Che schifo!

7 – Ti piace la scuola?
 – Dipende. Qualche volta sì, qualche volta no.
 – Ti piace oggi?
 – Oggi sì. Abbiamo italiano.

8 – Fai i compiti...ah sì! Tu fai i compiti dopo cena. Sempre, qual...?
 – Qualche volta. Qualche volta guardo la televisione.

9 – Parli italiano in classe?
 – Sì, sempre. Noi parliamo italiano sempre!
 – Sempre? Non parli inglese?
 – Qualche volta...ma solo un po' d'inglese.
 – Va bene, scrivo 4 punti.
 – 4? È possibile.

10 – E finalmente, fai il bravo a scuola?
 – Sì, sempre. Sono un angelo!
 – Tu? Qualche volta tu sei molto antipatico. Tu parli in classe, tu mangi in classe, tu giochi a basket in classe...
 – Va bene, va bene. Qualche volta non faccio il bravo.
 – Grazie. Il test è finito.
 – Prego. Arrivederci.

Sei un bravo ragazzo?
Sei una brava ragazza?

Nome _____ Età _____

Classe _____

test

		sempre	qualche volta	mai
1	Aiuti tuo padre o tua madre a casa?	☐	☐	☐
2	Fai il tuo letto?	☐	☐	☐
3	Fai la spesa?	☐	☐	☐
4	Prepari la cena?	☐	☐	☐
5	Fai i piatti dopo cena?	☐	☐	☐
6	Mangi la verdura a cena?	☐	☐	☐
7	Ti piace la scuola?	☐	☐	☐
8	Fai i compiti?	☐	☐	☐
9	Parli italiano in classe?	☐	☐	☐
10	Fai il bravo/la brava a casa e a scuola?	☐	☐	☐

**45–50 punti:
Sei un angelo!**

You're too good to be true. Loosen up and enjoy life!

**30–45 punti:
Sei bravissimo/a.**

You sound like a good kid. Keep it going!

**15–30 punti:
Sei bravo/a.**

You have room to improve but, hey, nobody's perfect.

**0–15 punti:
Sei un diavolo!**

You devil, you!

Una seconda lettera in Italia

Caro Scarno,

Grazie per la tua lettera! Anche tu guardi I Simpsons! Parlano inglese o italiano?

Hai una famiglia, Scarno? Hai fratelli e sorelle? Io ho due sorelle ma non ho fratelli. Jessica ha nove anni e Hannah ha tre anni.

Jessica è brava, ma qualche volta e antipatica. È molto pigra. Non aiuta mamma mai! Io aiuto mamma sempre, ma io sono un angelo!

Mi piace Hannah. È molto birichina. Parla sempre. È piccola ma mangia molto!

Mia madre ha trentasette anni. Si chiama Helen. Mamma è molto bella e molto simpatica. Gioca a tennis. Anche lei fa l'italiano a scuola.

Mio padre abita in un piccolo appartamento a Hawthorn. L'appartamento ha una camera da letto, un bagno, una piccola cucina e un piccolo salotto. Papà è molto simpatico. È spiritoso. Gioca a golf, ma non è molto bravo.

La mia casa ha quattro camere da letto, due bagni, un salotto e una sala da pranzo. Abbiamo anche un grande giardino. Tu hai una casa, o abiti a scuola?

Qualche volta mamma prepara la pasta per la cena. Mi piacciono gli spaghetti e le lasagne. La pasta è italiana, no? Ti piace? Ti piace la verdura?

Aspetto una seconda lettera, Scarno. Su! Forza!

Ciao!

Il tuo amico,
Travis

In the **io** column, give yourself a tick for each thing that you know how to do in Italian. Then ask a friend to check you and mark the **amico/a** column. Keep the last column free for when your teacher has time to hear how you are progressing.

Nome _____ **Classe** _____

Capitolo 3	io	amico/a	
Ask how many brothers and sisters someone has			
Say how many brothers and sisters you have			
Say what people in your family are like			
Say what sort of place you live in			
Talk about the different rooms at your place			
Talk about the things people do at your place			
Talk about people playing sports			
Talk about different pasta shapes			
Say which ones you like and which you don't			
Say who's cooking the pasta where			
Say whether it's cooked or not			
Say who's doing the sauce			
Say what it's like			
Carry out a survey about what people do			
Respond to a survey about what you do			
Tell someone to slow down			
Tell someone to get up			
Tell someone to wait			
Tell someone not to talk nonsense			
Tell someone they're an angel			
Tell someone they're a devil			

Capitolo 3

Suggested procedure

STAGE 1

• Preparatory activity

Introduce the topic of animals in general and pets in particular by bringing something into class to get the conversation going. The best thing to bring would be a pet that is not going to run amok: a goldfish or budgie should do the trick. Failing that, a rubber spider or snake might arouse some interest. Or you could pull a rabbit out of a hat. If realia are unavailable, you could bring a picture of your dog, cat or horse. If none of the above appeals, you could kick things off with some flash-cards.

Your introduction might go something like this: **Questo è il mio pesce. Si chiama Pierluigi. Ha due anni. Ti piace? È molto simpatico. Io amo i pesci. Poveretto, sta male. È ammalato oggi. Non mangia.**
Ti piacciono gli animali? Hai un animale a casa? Quanti animali domestici hai tu?

For the next series of lessons, encourage students to bring in their own pets, or photos thereof, and to present them to the class. They should be happy to take questions about them.

If you have not already introduced the rubber spider as your pet, you could plant it in the classroom and then happen upon it: **Aiii, un ragno!!! Che schifo, odio i ragni!!** Or you could handle it lovingly and put it on the desk of an unsuspecting student: **Questo è il mio ragno, Romolo. Che fifone! Hai paura di Romolo? Non ti piacciono i ragni?** If you are ideologically opposed to animals in the classroom you might get some mileage from a computer mouse: **Aiuto! Un topo! Che schifo! Ho paura dei topi.**

Build up a list of words and expressions on the board once your students have heard them in use in the classroom.

• In poche parole 1A Textbook p 60

First, practise saying the names of the animals, as labelled in the illustration. Then use this exercise to drill the basic 'animal' vocabulary of this chapter. Initially, students could respond referring to the vocabulary list on page 59 of the *Textbook*. Then they could try it without looking at the list.

After the class has completed this exercise, you could set the vocabulary from **Impariamo le parole!** on page 59 of the *Textbook*, from **l'animale** to **il veterinario**, for learning by heart.

• In poche parole 1B Textbook p 60

You might like to foreshadow the work on ancient Rome later in the chapter by asking if anyone knows who Remo has named his spider after. If nobody else can, you might go on to tell the story of the abandoned twins, Romulus and Remus, who were rescued from the banks of the Tiber by a she-wolf. The wolf raised the boys until they were ready to make their own way in the world. They explored the area around the Tiber looking for a suitable site for a new city. In 753 BC, Romulus thought that he had found one and began building the wall that would be its boundary. Remus mocked his brother and his new city site by jumping over the wall. Romulus naturally killed Remus and became the undisputed ruler of a new city that still bears his name.

• Penna in mano! D Quanti animali!
Workbook p 56

• Dal veterinario Textbook p 56

Listen to and read this story, allowing your students to enjoy and respond to it as a whole. Then return to the first page for a repeat run-through of the first six frames to prepare the class for the first set of comprehension questions.

After the class has completed this first reading, you could set the vocabulary from **Impariamo le parole!** on page 59 of the *Textbook,* from **allegro** to **fuori**, for learning by heart.

• Penna in mano! A Vero o falso?
Workbook p 54

• Domande Textbook p 59

Concentrate on questions 1 to 7.

• Penna in mano! B Perchè? Perchè!
Workbook p 54

- **Studiamo la lingua! A Andare**
  Workbook p 63

- **Su con l'orecchio! A Dal veterinario**
  Workbook p 50, Cassette 3, tape script Teacher's Manual p 38

As in previous chapters, return to the tape script once the basic exercise has been successfully completed by your class. See if they can tell you:

1 Why this is a particularly smart parrot.
2 Why this is not a particularly smart fish owner.
3 Why the snake left the clinic untreated.
4 Why the rabbit is getting sick.
5 What is causing the vet to sneeze.
6 What problem the vet is having with the spider.
7 How the dog and the vet feel about each other.
8 What happened to the mouse.

- **Rompicapi A Fungo il fifone**
  Workbook p 66

Solution: Fungo's greatest fear is the **veterinario**.

STAGE 2

- **Dal veterinario** *Textbook p 56*

Listen to and read the story again. Encourage your students to role-play the different character parts.

After the class has completed this first reading, you could set the vocabulary from **Impariamo le parole!** on page 59 of the *Textbook*, from **amare** to **avere paura di**, for learning by heart.

- **Domande** *Textbook p 59*

Concentrate on questions 8 to 14.

- **Penna in mano! C Dal veterinario: Domande** *Workbook p 55*

- **In poche parole 1C** *Textbook p 61*

Obviously, exercises which allow for alternative answers are harder to drill with the whole class. If you decide that you need to practise it in this way you will have to come to a consensus: 'O.K., this time through we'll say that we *do* like all the animals pictured here'. You may decide to skip this phase and ask individual students or have the class do this exercise and the next in pairs.

- **In poche parole 1D** *Textbook p 61*

To meet the communicative demands of this chapter, your students are required to say things like: **Ha paura *del* veterinario. Non ho paura *dei* ragni.** Don't be tempted to go into a full-blown lesson on 'articulated prepositions' at this point. For the time being, the brief explanation in the **Studiamo la lingua!** section is quite adequate. This grammar topic will be taken up again at a later date.

- **Studiamo la lingua! C Che fifone!**
  Workbook p 64

- **Penna in mano! E Ami o odi?**
  Workbook p 57

After the class has completed this exercise, you could set the vocabulary from **Impariamo le parole!** on page 59 of the *Textbook*, from **adesso** to **scappa!**, for learning by heart.

- **A tu per tu 1** *Textbook p 64*

Once they have had time to practise, ask pairs of students to perform their dialogue for the rest of the class.

- **Ti piacciono gli animali?**
  Textbook p 62

Note that two words for 'happy' are introduced in this chapter: **allegro** and **contento**. And there is another referred to in the advertisement for cat food: whereas the fish are **sani e allegri**, the cats are **felini e contenti** (a pun on **felici e contenti**).

Does anyone know of a famous cartoon cat who is always **felice** (as well as **felino**)?

- **Penna in mano! F Ti piacciono gli animali?** *Workbook p 57*

- **Rompicapi B Al contrario**
  Workbook p 66

- **Su con l'orecchio! B L'hit parade degli animali** *Workbook p 51, Cassette 3, tape script Teacher's Manual p 39*

Use this listening exercise as an example your students can follow when they do the survey themselves.

- **A lingua sciolta! L'hit parade degli animali** *Textbook p 65, repromaster Teacher's Manual p 43*

The animal hit parade can be established by collating the results of the surveys done by the students. Perhaps the simplest way is to ask students for results and register them on the board: **Va bene, cominciamo per i cani. Chi ha cinque punti per i cani?** (multiply the number of students by five) **Chi ha tre punti?** etc. Once you have the total number of points for each animal you can put them in order of popularity.

STAGE 3

- *Un giro di Roma con Antonio*
  Textbook p 67

Before you start this guided tour of Rome, find out what your students already know about the Eternal City:

1 Why does it attract tourists from all over the world?

2 What famous things in Rome have you heard of? (Of course, the Vatican is an important part of Rome's universal appeal. This will be dealt with in a later chapter.)

Listen to and read through the **fotoromanzo**. You will not want to bog the class down in historical detail but you can afford to give some interesting background material as the tour unfolds. Aim to impart some of the more memorable facts:

- **The Colosseum**

  This fantastic stadium dates back to 72 AD. It held 50 000 spectators. (How does that compare with your local stadium?) People of all classes used to flock to it to see the gladiators fight each other to the death. Sometimes the arena was flooded to allow mock sea battles to be waged. Wild beasts were also brought into the arena to take their chances with the gladiators. Stories about Christians being fed to the lions are thought to be the stuff of legend rather than history. These days the Colosseum, as well as being a major tourist drawcard, is the centre of a huge traffic island and the home of countless cats.

- **The Roman Forum**

  This was the CBD of ancient Rome and included the main government buildings and temples. Although it is in ruins today, archaeologists have been able to identify each of the sites. It is full of atmosphere and is a great place for the sound and light shows that recreate the era of the Roman Empire.

- **The Circus Maximus**

  Surely everyone has seen those epic films that featured chariots hurtling around this huge racetrack? It could once hold 200 000 spectators.

- **The Palatine Hill**

  This is the hill on which, according to legend, Romulus founded the city. It provides lovely views over the Roman Forum and the Circus Maximus. It also catches some of the fresh breezes on a hot Roman summer evening. No wonder it was a favourite place for the rich and famous of ancient Rome to build their palaces.

- **The Castel Sant'Angelo**

  In this part of Rome we are a few kilometres from the ancient centre, quite close to the Vatican. Hundreds of years after the fall of the Roman Empire, when Rome was governed by popes, this castle was the main Vatican fortress. There is still a secret passageway linking the castle with the pope's apartment in the Vatican, just in case he needs to make a quick get-away.

- **The Victor Emmanuel monument**

  This is really modern, having been built in 1911! Until 1870 Italy was not really a country but a collection of separate states (including the one governed by the Pope). Vittorio Emanuele II was king of **Piemonte**, a state in the northern part of Italy. He sent Garibaldi all the way down to Sicily with just 1000 men to force the government there to become part of a united Italy. Garibaldi then moved up to Rome to force the pope to join this new, united country as well.

  Many people are critical of this monument. Can anyone in the class suggest why? One of its nicknames is the Wedding Cake.

- *Penna in mano! G Un giro di Roma antica Workbook p 58*

- *Su con l'orecchio! C Un giro di Roma Workbook p 52, Cassette 3, tape script Teacher's Manual p 40*

Once the basic exercise has been successfully completed by your class, you could try your class with these supplementary questions. See if they can tell you:

1 How many other castles there are to be seen in Rome.

2 What the passenger did once they were within view of the Colosseum.

3 What he finds hard to believe about the Colosseum.

4 When Antonio likes to come to the Roman Forum.

5 What the passenger first thought the Circus Maximus.

6 What he wanted to see there.

7 The joke the passenger made about the Palatine.

8 How the passenger feels about the Victor Emmanuel monument.

- *Studiamo la lingua! B Bravissimo!*
  Workbook p 63

- *In poche parole 3A* *Textbook p 73*

- *In poche parole 3B* *Textbook p 73*

For those having difficulty working out what's what in the illustration, the following list will solve your problems: 1 **la chiesa** 2 **il monumento** 3 **la statua** 4 **il palazzo** 5 **la fontana** 6 **la piazza** 7 **il gatto**

- *Penna in mano! H Una città italiana*
  Workbook p 59

- *Studiamo la lingua! B Molti!*
  Workbook p 64

STAGE 4

- *Il corpo* *Textbook p 70*

This is a photographic vocabulary presentation that continues the mood of monumental Rome. This assortment of body parts is housed in the courtyard of one of the **palazzi** surrounding **il Campidoglio**, Michelangelo's square atop the Capitoline Hill. Like the Palatine Hill, the Capitoline overlooks the Roman Forum.

You probably have your own tried and true methods of teaching parts of the body. You don't have to rely on the statues, of course; your classroom is full of live exhibits. Perhaps you could ask some of the more lively exhibits to become statues for the purposes of drilling this vocabulary.

You could ask the class to repeat the words after you, then move on to ask them **Che cos'è? È l'orecchio?** They might enjoy a game of **Simone dice.** If you are having difficulty reducing the number of those still 'in', try distracting them by saying **Simone dice 'tocca la spalla!'** as you reach down to clasp one of your own knees.

- *Penna in mano! I Il corpo*
  Textbook p 60

- *Rompicapi C Che corpo!*
  Workbook p 67

Solution: 1 **pancia** 2 **petto** 3 **ombelico** 4 **testa** 5 **capelli** 6 **dito** 7 **piede** 8 **occhio** 9 **naso** 10 **braccio** 11 **mano**

- *In poche parole 2A* *Textbook p 71*

For this exercise and the next, your students are required to speak to and for the characters. This will enable them to practise the language they need, to talk about their own ailments (and to avoid more complicated forms of indirect object pronouns.)

- *In poche parole 2B* *Textbook p 71*

- *Penna in mano! J Dal medico*
  Workbook p 61

- *A tu per tu* *Textbook p 72*

This exercise is a little different from others of its type in that it introduces some new vocabulary. (Labelling **il dente** and **la gola** on the statues proved to be a little tricky!) Some students may notice the irregular masculine noun **il dentista.** Praise them for their alertness and encourage them to accept it at face value: 'Well yes, there are a few that don't follow the normal pattern.' The same sort of comment could be made in reference to **la mano.** It would be a shame to interrupt the flow of language and become unduly preoccupied with grammatical exceptions. The plural forms of the body parts will be followed up at a later stage of the course.

- *Su con l'orecchio! D Dal medico*
  Workbook p 52, Cassette 3, tape script Teacher's Manual p 40

Once the exercise has been successfully completed by your class, you could try your class with these supplementary questions. See if they can tell you:

1. The mistake the doctor made about the sport Carmelo plays.
2. Why Carmelo was so disappointed.
3. Why Angela squealed.
4. Why the doctor's mind wasn't on the job with his golfing patient.
5. The difficulty he was having with Sandro, the rugby player.
6. What the doctor found interesting about the aerobics injury.
7. Which team the basketballer faced next.
8. Why the doctor called him a **fifone**.

• *Rompicapi D Troviamo le parole!*
Workbook p 67

Your students will soon discover that there are more than 45 words and a definite article to be found here. You can challenge them with the cryptic clue that even though there are 47 words in the puzzle, there are only 43 animals, body parts and Italian city sights in total.
Solution: 1 **topo** 2 **animale domestico**
3 **cavallo** 4 **animale** 5 **gatto** 6 **ragno**
7 **uccello** 8 **coniglio** 9 **tartarughe** 10 **pesce**
11 **serpente** 12 **pappagallo** 13 **cane**
14 **piccione** 15 **centro** 16 **città** 17 **statua**
18 **palazzo** 19 **piazza** 20 **monumento**
21 **chiesa** 22 **fontana** 23 **negozio** 24 **carro**
25 **il** 26 **naso** 27 **corpo** 28 **ombelico** 29 **petto**
30 **collo** 31 **gamba** 32 **gola** 33 **mano** 34 **testa**
35 **bocca** 36 **dente** 37 **pancia** 38 **dito**
39 **braccio** 40 **capelli** 41 **faccia** 42 **dito del piede** 43 **orecchio** 44 **piede**

• *Il latino* Textbook p 69

This extra cultural reading takes up the theme of ancient Rome again. There are a few words and grammatical forms that your students have not seen before, but encourage them to use what they do know and some intelligent guesswork to work out what they mean. The English word 'inscription' may be unfamiliar to many of them, so this is their chance to learn it!

There is obviously scope for amplifying the content of this brief passage through some class discussion. The fact that Latin is the main source of several Romance languages will be of interest.

The bubbles to the three punks give you the chance to tell your class about Julius Caesar's famous boast upon his conquest of Britain: *Veni, vidi, vici.* Your students have already encountered **vieni** and **venite** and in this chapter they meet **vedere**. They will deal with **vincere** in **Capitolo 5**.

(Note: In *Avanti!*, pages 155–6, there is some more detail about Latin and an interesting table that your students would enjoy completing.)

• *Su con l'orecchio! E Che fifoni!*
Workbook p 53, Cassette 3, tape script Teacher's Manual p 41

• *Studiamo la lingua! E I verbi sono simpatici* Workbook p 65

• *Studiamo la lingua! F Amo i verbi*
Workbook p 65

• *Rompicapi E No, non qui!*
Workbook p 68

• *Su con l'orecchio! F L'intervista*
Workbook p 53, Cassette 3, tape script Teacher's Manual p 42

This listening exercise assembles most of the topics and much of the language that your students have been dealing with in the first half of *Forza! uno*. The aim is not to intimidate but to draw together threads from the first four chapters and to impress them with the amount of language they can understand.

Students will probably require the interview to be played several times so that they can add to their notes each time they listen. Another approach would be to stop the tape after each topic has been covered. Students should be allowed to make their notes under the headings in English or Italian, or in a mixture of both.

The correction session will be invaluable, as students are given the opportunity to reconstitute the text by contributing the pieces that they have understood.

• *Penna in mano! K L'intervista*
Workbook p 62

Now that they have heard an extended interview your class should be well placed to tackle one of their own. The first stage, as suggested in the instruction in the *Textbook*, is to prepare it in writing. The pictorial prompting is meant to remind students of topics they have covered and questions they know how to ask, without imposing a particular structure.

- *L'intervista* Textbook p 75

This is the **A lingua sciolta!** activity for **Capitolo 4.** Your students will undoubtedly enjoy performing their interview for the rest of the class.

- *Rompicapi F Cruciverba* Workbook p 69

Solution:

Suggested assessment tasks

Listening

- *Su con l'orecchio! B L'hit parade degli animali* Workbook p 51, Cassette 3, tape script Teacher's Manual p 39

- *Su con l'orecchio! C Un giro di Roma* Workbook p 52, Cassette 3, tape script Teacher's Manual p 40

- *Su con l'orecchio! F L'intervista* Workbook p 53, Cassette 3, tape script Teacher's Manual p 42

Speaking

- *In poche parole 1A and B* Textbook p 60

- *A tu per tu 1* Textbook p 64

- *A tu per tu 2* Textbook p 72

- *L'intervista* Textbook p 75

Reading

- *Penna in mano! A Vero o falso?* Workbook p 54

- *Penna in mano! C Dal Veterinario: Domande* Workbook p 55

Writing

- *Penna in mano! E Ami o odi?* Workbook p 57

- *Penna in mano! F Ti piacciono gli animali?* Workbook p 57

- *Penna in mano! G Un giro di Roma antica* Workbook p 58

- *Penna in mano! J Dal medico* Workbook p 61

Su con l'orecchio! Tape scripts

A Dal veterinario

In what order did the vet see the animals? Write the appropriate number next to each one.

1 – Come sta l'uccello, signore?
  – Molto male, dottore.
  – Molto male, dottore.
  – Come, molto male?
  – Poveretto, non mangia.
  – Poveretto, non mangia...cioè, non mangio.
  – Sta zitto, tu!
  – Sta zitto, tu!
  – Uffa!

2 – Chi è il prossimo? Ah, buongiorno, signore.
  – Buongiorno, dottore. È ammalato. È ammalatissimo.
  – Mmm. Questo pesce non è ammalato.
  – No? Non è ammalato?
  – No, è morto.
  – Morto?
  – Ma sì, è un pesce. È fuori d'acqua.
  – Ooooo.
  – Uffa!

3 – Aiii, fuori, fuori! Subito!

– Ma è ammalato, dottore.

– Via, fuori! Ho paura dei serpenti.

– Vieni, Silvestro. Questo veterinario è un fifone!

4 – Questo coniglio sta male. Che cosa mangia?

– Mangia farfalle, dottore.

– Farfalle?

– Sì, e spaghetti e lasagne...

– Ma è un coniglio. I conigli mangiano la verdura, non la pasta!

– Ma il mio coniglio odia la verdura.

– Uffa!

5 – Eccì! Atciù!

– Salute, dottore.

– Grazie. Mi dispiace, ma è il gatto...ecciù!

– Il gatto? Ma come?

– È un'allergia. Sono allergica ai gatti.

– Un veterinario allergico ai gatti?! Mamma mia!

– Eccì! Atciù!

6 – Che schifo! Un ragno! Odio i ragni!

– Ma dottore, è ammalato.

– Sì, che cosa c'è?

– È la gamba dottore.

– Questa gamba?

– No, dottore.

– Questa gamba?

– No, dottore.

– Questa?

– No...

7 – Vieni! Forza, coraggio! Vieni!

– Che cos'è? Perchè non entra?

– È il mio cane, dottore. Ha paura del veterinario.

– Meno male. Io ho paura dei cani.

8 – Buongiorno.

– Buongiorno, dottore. Il mio topo sta male.

– Mmm, vediamo un po'. Ma no, vieni qui...

– Il mio topo. È morto!

– Mi dispiace, la trappola...

– È morto. Assassina! Assassina!

– Uffa!

B L'hit parade degli animali

Listen as these students do the survey **L'hit parade degli animali**. Fill in the details at the top of the form and then complete it by ticking the appropriate columns and entering a score for each animal.

– Sei pronto?

– Sì, sono pronto. Avanti!

– Va bene. Nome?

– Scusa?

– Il tuo nome! Come ti chiami?

– Remo.

– Età?

– Come?

– Età! Quanti anni hai?

– Quasi quattordici.

– Quasi quattordici? Hai tredici anni, allora. In che classe sei?

– 8B.

– Grazie. Quali animali domestici hai tu?

– Ho una giraffa.

– Spiritoso! Hai un animale?

– No.

– Qual è il tuo animale preferito?

– La giraffa.

– Va bene. Adesso facciamo queste domande. Ti piacciono i cani?

– No.

– No?? Odi i cani?

– No, non odio i cani, ma non mi piacciono, ecco.

– I cavalli?

– Sì, mi piacciono.

– Ti piacciono i conigli?

– Amo i conigli. Sono molto buoni.

– Buoni? Come buoni?

– Mangio i conigli e sono molto buoni.

– Va bene, 5 punti per i conigli. Mangi anche i gatti?

– No. Odio i gatti.

– Odi i gatti? Perchè? Sono simpatici.

– I gatti? Sono antipaticissimi!!!

– I pappagalli?

– Mi piacciono i pappagalli perchè parlano. Sono intelligenti.

- Ti piacciono i pesci?
- No.
- Perchè no?
- Non so.
- Ti piacciono i piccioni?
- Amo i piccioni. Mio padre ha molti piccioni a casa. Sono fantastici!
- Sì?
- Sì! Volano cento, duecento chilometri ma sempre tornano a casa!
- Ti piacciono i ragni?
- Non molto.
- I serpenti?
- No! Odio i serpenti! Ho paura dei serpenti!
- Le tartarughe ti piacciono?
- Sì...sì.
- E i topi?
- No, odio i topi. Abbiamo topi a casa.
- Non hai un gatto? I gatti mangiano i topi.
- Sì, ma odio anche i gatti.
- Uffa! Grazie. È finito.
- Prego. Arrivederci.

C Un giro di Roma antica

In what order did Antonio show his taxi passengers the sights of Rome? Write the appropriate number next to each place.

1 - Come si chiama il castello?
  - Dove?
  - A destra.
  - Ah, è il Castel Sant'Angelo. È bello, no?
  - È bellissimo.

2 - A sinistra c'è il Tevere.
  - Il fiume?
  - Il fiume, sì.
  - Mmm, è bello.
  - Be', non c'è male.

3 - Come si chiama il monumento bianco?
  - È il monumento a Vittorio Emanuele.
  - Un monumento bianco qui a Roma! Non mi piace!
  - No? È brutto?
  - No, non è brutto, è...è...non so, non mi piace, ecco!

4 - A destra vediamo il Foro Romano.

- Il Foro Romano! Che bello!
- Mi piace di sera. È bellissimo.
- Va bene, vengo qui di sera.

5 - Ecco il Colosseo!
  - Dove, dove?
  - Ecco, in fondo.
  - Ah, è fantastico. Faccio una fotografia!
  - Va bene, io aspetto qui.
  - Grazie. Quanti anni ha il Colosseo?
  - Quasi duemila.
  - Duemila anni! Non ci credo!

6 - Che cos'è? Lo Stadio Olimpico?
  - Ma no! È il Circo Massimo.
  - Ah, questo è il Circo Massimo. Ma dove sono i carri? Dove sono i cavalli?
  - Be', non so.

7 - Questa è Piazza della Repubblica.
  - È molto grande.
  - È una grande piazza, sì.
  - Ci sono piccioni in Piazza della Repubblica?
  - Qualche volta, sì.

8 - Come si chiama la fontana?
  - La fontana?
  - La fontana in Piazza della Repubblica.
  - Be', non so. Ci sono molte fontane a Roma.

9 - E questa fontana?
  - Aah, questa fontana è famosissima!
  - Non è la Fontana di Trevi?!
  - È la Fontana di Trevi.
  - Caspita! È bellissima!
  - Eh sì! Vuole fare una fotografia?

D Dal medico

These sportswomen and men are visiting the sports medicine clinic in Rome. Help the doctor keep his records up-to-date by highlighting the part of the body that is injured and the sport in which the people are involved.

1 - Buongiorno, Carmelo.
  - Buongiorno, dottore.
  - Allora, che c'è oggi?
  - La gamba, dottore. Mi fa male la gamba.
  - Destra o sinistra?

– Destra.

– Mmm. E tu giochi a tennis, no?

– Squash. Gioco a squash. Gioco domani nel campionato di Roma.

– Mi dispiace, Carmelo, ma tu non giochi domani.

– Uffa!

2 – Buonasera, Angela. Come va la tua squadra di hockey?

– Benissimo, dottore. Ma io non sto molto bene.

– No? Che cos'hai?

– È questo braccio, dottore. Mi fa male.

– Mmm, il braccio destro. Ti fa male qui?

– Aiii! Sì, mi fa male lì!

– Mi dispiace, Angela.

3 – Allora, che c'è che non va?

– Questa spalla mi fa male, dottore.

– La spalla destra? E che sport pratichi tu?

– Gioco a golf.

– Il golf? Ah, mi piace il golf. Guardo sempre il golf alla televisione. Ti piace Greg Norman?

– Sì, mi piace. La mia spalla, dottore?

– Ah sì, la tua spalla. Vediamo un po'.

4 – Buongiorno, Sandro. Che cosa hai, oggi?

– Prego, dottore?

– Che cosa hai? Che cosa c'è?

– Ah, mi dispiace. È l'orecchio. Mi fa male l'orecchio.

– Destro o sinistro?

– Prego, dottore?

– Destro o sinistro?

– Destro.

– Tu giochi a rugby, vero?

– No, dottore, gioco a rugby.

– Come?

– Prego?

– Uffa!

5 – Aiii!

– Ti fa male?

– Sì, dottore.

– Dove?

– Qui.

– Qui?

– No, qui.

– Ah, il collo. Interessante! Tu fai la ginnastica, vero?

– Be', è un tipo di ginnastica. Faccio l'aerobica.

– Anch'io faccio l'aerobica! Anche il mio collo fa male!

– Interessante!

6 – Come va la tua squadra di basket?

– Non c'è male. Giochiamo contro Firenze stasera.

– Firenze! Loro sono forti. E tu, che cos'hai?

– È il piede sinistro, dottore. Mi fa male.

– Il piede ti fa male?

– È il dito del piede. Questo qui.

– Poveretto! Il dito del piede ti fa male. Ti faccio un'iniezione!

– Un'iniezione! No, dottore!

– Non fare il fifone!

E Che fifoni!

What are these people afraid of? Write a number under the appropriate illustration to show that you have understood.

1 – Aii!

– Che cosa c'è?

– Mi fa male questo dente.

– Perchè non vai dal dentista, allora?

– No, non mi piace il dentista.

– Perchè no? Hai paura del dentista?

– Sì.

– Che fifone!

2 – Ciao! Sono quasi pronta. Avanti! Avanti!

– No, grazie. Aspetto qui fuori.

– Non dire stupidaggini. Avanti! Vieni dentro!

– No, aspetto qui.

– Perchè…è Fungo? Ma è simpaticissimo!

– Ci credo, ma ho paura dei cani.

– Hai paura dei cani?! Va bene. Un momento, vengo subito.

3 – Non ci credo! Non guardi la televisione! Fai i compiti!

– Faccio sempre i compiti di storia.

– Perchè?

– È il nuovo professore. È severissimo.

– Aah, hai paura del professore!

– Sì, un po'.

4 – Aiii! Aiuto!

– Che c'è?

– Guarda! Guarda!

– Che cosa?

– Lì, dietro il letto! Un ragno!

– Hai paura dei ragni?! Ma i ragni non fanno male. Mangiano le mosche.

– Che schifo! Io non vado in camera da letto con un ragno!

5 – Scusa, hai paura dei serpenti?

– Io? No.

– Benissimo. Ecco, guarda, questo è il mio serpente. Si chiama Silvestro.

– Via, via! Sei matto? Aiuto! Aiuto!

– Non hai paura dei serpenti?! Che fifone!

6 – Ma tu sei un pesce fuori d'acqua! Perchè non vieni nell'acqua?

– Ho paura dei pescecani!

– Hai paura dei pesci e dei cani?!

– No, dei pescecani. Degli squali.

– Non ci sono pescecani qui.

– Non ci credo.

F L'intervista

Gino is taping an interview for the school radio station with a student who has just arrived from Italy. You want to write an article about her for the school newspaper, so you get down as much information as you can. You can use the headings below as a guide.

– Ah, buongiorno. Siediti! Come stai?

– Non c'è male. Ho mal di gola oggi.

– Ah, poveretta! Sei pronta per l'intervista? Ho molte domande.

– Sì, sono pronta. Avanti!

– Allora, come ti chiami?

– Mi chiamo Franca Stefanelli.

– Quanti anni hai, Franca?

– Ho tredici anni.

– E dove abiti?

– Abito a Sorrento.

– Ti piace?

– Sì, è una bellissima città.

– Com'è la tua casa?

– Non è una casa, è un appartamento.

– Va bene, com'è il tuo appartamento?

– Ha due camere da letto. Non è grande, ma è bello. Mi piace.

– Hai fratelli o sorelle?

– Ho un fratello e una sorella.

– Quanti anni hanno?

– Mio fratello ha quindici anni e mia sorella ha diciassette anni.

– E come sono?

– Mio fratello è molto sportivo. Gioca a basket e a cricket. Mia sorella gioca a tennis. Anche lei è sportiva.

– E tu?

– Come?

– E tu? Sei sportiva anche tu?

– No, non molto.

– Pratichi uno sport?

– Gioco un po' a beach volley.

– Sei brava?

– Non sono brava, ma mi piace.

– Benissimo! Aiuti tuo padre o tua madre a casa?

– Un po'. Faccio il mio letto e faccio i piatti dopo cena. E qualche volta lavoro in giardino.

– Brava! Hai animali domestici?

– Abbiamo un gatto a casa. Si chiama Goffredo. Ha dodici anni.

– Ti piacciono i gatti?

– Sì, molto. Amo i gatti. Sono simpaticissimi.

– Allora, il gatto è il tuo animale preferito?

– Mmm, non so. Non ho un animale preferito.

– Ti piace la scuola?

– Sì, molto. Amo la scuola.

– Ami la scuola? Non ci credo. Perchè?

– È molto interessante.

– Va bene. Adesso parliamo di musica. Che tipo di musica ti piace?

– Mi piace la musica moderna. Amo il rap.

– Che schifo! Ah scusa! Mi dispiace! Senti, guardi la televisione a casa?

– Non molto. Non mi piace la televisione.

– No? Perchè no? Non è divertente?

– No, è noiosa.

– Molto interessante! Grazie.

– L'intervista è finita?

– Sì, è finita. Grazie.

– Prego.

L'hit parade degli animali

Nome _____

Età _____ **Classe** _____

Quali animali domestici hai tu?

_____

Qual è il tuo animale preferito?

_____

	Amo	Mi piacciono	Non mi piacciono	Odio	*Punti*	*Classe*
	☐	☐	☐	☐	☐	☐
	☐	☐	☐	☐	☐	☐
	☐	☐	☐	☐	☐	☐
	☐	☐	☐	☐	☐	☐
	☐	☐	☐	☐	☐	☐
	☐	☐	☐	☐	☐	☐
	☐	☐	☐	☐	☐	☐
	☐	☐	☐	☐	☐	☐
	☐	☐	☐	☐	☐	☐
	☐	☐	☐	☐	☐	☐
	☐	☐	☐	☐	☐	☐

Score the answers as follows:

Amo	5 punti
Mi piacciono	3 punti
Non mi piacciono	1 punti
Odio	0 punti

In the **io** column, give yourself a tick for each thing that you know how to do in Italian. Then ask a friend to check you and mark the **amico/a** column. Keep the last column free for when your teacher has time to hear how you are progressing.

Nome _____ **Classe** _____

Capitolo 4	io	amico/a	
Ask people about their pets			
Talk about your own pets			
Talk about animals you like			
Talk about animals you dislike or hate			
Talk about animals you're scared of			
Say where you're going			
Say you're going to someone's place			
Say whether you're inside or outside			
Name different parts of the body			
Say that you're sick			
Ask someone what's wrong			
Say what's wrong with you			
Say you're feeling better			
Say your head, throat etc is better			
Say that someone or something is extremely...			
Say that you're sick of something			
Tell someone to get going			
Tell someone not to act like a wimp			
Cry out for help			
Identify different features of an Italian city			
Recognise some sights around Rome			

Suggested procedure

STAGE 1

- **Non c'è niente da fare!**
  Textbook p 76

Listen to and read this story, encouraging students to use the visual material to help them understand new words and expressions. Once they have enjoyed the story as a whole, listen to and read the first two pages again.

The action of this story takes place on Sunday. For the purposes of this chapter, **domenica** occurs as a single item of vocabulary which recurs in the section on **il calcio**. The other day of the week that is mentioned is **venerdì** which occurs in the **Luneur** poster attached to **A tu per tu**. There is no real need to do so, but you may decide that it is high time to teach (or revise, as the case may be) **i giorni della settimana**.

Some of your students will have seen *Il Re Leone* and be pleased to tell you about it. You could bite the communicative bullet and start asking them about it: **Chi ha visto *Il Re Leone*? Com'è? È bello, interessante, divertente, noioso? È un film per bambini? Che tipo di film è? Ti piacciono i cartoni animati?** Those who have seen it may be able to work out the text on the publicity poster: **L'avventura più grande è trovare il tuo posto nel cerchio della vita.**

- **Domande 1–10** *Textbook p 81*

- **Penna in mano! A Non c'è niente da fare! I** *Workbook p 74*

- **In poche parole 1A** *Textbook p 82*

Make sure that you give the cues for this exercise so that the students will hear you classify the characters (**uomo, donna, ragazzo, ragazza, topo**) and identify what they are doing. In the first instance, their response could simply be a name: **È Antonio**. Having done the exercise at this basic level, they can repeat it, adding the extra information: **È Antonio, il padre di Francesco**. The characters can be related to Francesco, except Francesco himself (**il fratello di Lucio**) and Gigio (**il topo di Antonella**). Antonella is **l'amica di Lucio**.

- **In poche parole 1B** *Textbook p 82*

- **Penna in mano! B Chi sono e che cosa fanno?** *Workbook p 75*

For those having trouble recognising her in black and white and without her mouse, the girl in the last frame is Antonella.

- **Su con l'orecchio! A Non c'è niente da fare!** *Workbook p 70, Cassette 4, tape script Teacher's Manual p 48*

As in previous chapters, return to the tape script once the basic exercise has been successfully completed by your class. See if your students can tell you:

1 Why Laura's mother is surprised that she would go to the park to skate.
2 What Paolo's parent thinks of his choice of activity.
3 What the guitarist promises his father.
4 Why mum is a bit exasperated.
5 Why Gina says that mum is **spiritosa**.
6 Why dad is a bit exasperated.

- **In poche parole 1C** *Textbook p 82*

There will be some more work on **volere** later in the chapter. For the time being, it is enough to explain that **voglio** means 'I want' and that it is followed by the part of the verb that means 'to...'. The only -ere verb here is **leggere**, which is given in the sample dialogue. Up to now the class has seen **vendere** and **vedere**.

- **A tu per tu** *Textbook p 84*

LUNEUR is the name given to Rome's Luna Park, since it is in the area of Rome called EUR. Ask the students why, according to the poster, is it good to make Friday the day you go out to **LUNEUR**?

You get a glimpse of EUR from the train window as you travel into town from the airport. There is another glimpse in the section in this chapter on **il calcio**: you will see a photo of boys practising their soccer in a park with a typical EUR building in the background.

(Note: In *Sempre Avanti!*, page 86, there is a photograph of one of **LUNEUR**'s attractions.)

- *Studiamo la lingua! B Volere*
  Workbook p 84

Most examples of forms of **volere** in this chapter are singular, with **voglio** and **vuoi** occurring in the story and **A tu per tu** while **vuole** features in the **Domande**. There is also an example of **volete** in the story. The class will meet **vogliono** in the section on **Videogiochi**.

- *Rompicapi B Troviamo le parole!*
  Workbook p 87

Solution: 1 **giornale** 2 **rivista** 3 **genitore** 4 **guanto** 5 **stadio** 6 **viola** 7 **eroe** 8 **rosso** 9 **senza** 10 **vincere** 11 **piscina** 12 **pallone** 13 **che** 14 **ascoltare** 15 **cinema** 16 **troppo** 17 **parco** 18 **disegnare** 19 **arrivare** 20 **blu** 21 **donna** 22 **uomo** 23 **altro** 24 **benvenuto**

The hidden phrase: **Che noia!**

STAGE 2

- *Preparatory activity*

Relaunch the theme of playing music and singing via some class discussion: **Chi suona uno strumento musicale? Che cosa suoni? La chitarra acustica o elettrica? Ah, la chitarra bassa. Sai cantare mentre suoni? Hai una canzone preferita?**

As well as the instruments mentioned in the story, you will probably need to talk about **il flauto** for all those who learned the recorder. **Maestri** and **maestre** of the glockenspiel, tambourine, bell and triangle can be told that they play **strumenti di percussione** but you may need to be more specific for exponents of **la batteria**. You will be only too pleased to pass on the name of any other instrument to satisfy your students.

- *Non c'è niente da fare!*
  Textbook p 76

Listen to and read the story once again. Encourage students to role-play the character parts. Concentrate this time on the second half of the story.

You could teach **destro** and **sinistro** and then ask these questions based on the picture of the boys playing Twister:

1 **Chi ha la mano sinistra su un punto azzurro?**

2 **Dov'è il piede sinistro di Lucio?**
3 **Dov'è la mano sinistra di Francesco?**
4 **Dov'è la mano destra di Lucio?**

- *Domande 11–20* Textbook p 81

- *Penna in mano! C Non c'è niente da fare! II* Workbook p 76

- *In poche parole 2A* Textbook p 83

The format of this exercise is slightly different from the norm in that there is no variable in the cue utterance: **Che noia! Non c'è niente da fare.** Whoever is saying this line can concentrate on sounding bored and frustrated. A suitable tone of exasperation needs to be injected into the reply: **Non dire stupidaggini!**

- *In poche parole 2B* Textbook p 83

- *Studiamo la lingua! A Perchè non mi piace!* Workbook p 84

- *Rompicapi A Diverse cose* Workbook p 86

- *Penna in mano! D Ti piace fare queste cose?* Workbook p 77

- *Penna in mano! E Parliamo di te!* Workbook p 78

STAGE 3

- *Viva il calcio!* Textbook p 85

Listen to and read through this photo-presentation. Note the boys training at EUR, just around the corner from Luna Park. The Sunday match is taking place in a small town in southern Tuscany. The **giallorosso** flag is flying outside one of the most expensive hotels on **Via Veneto** in Rome. The **biancoceleste** flags were on sale outside the **Olimpico** on the day of **il derby**. Do your students know when the Olympic Games were held in Rome? Notice **la lupa**, mascot of the Roman football club. Does anyone in your class remember a story involving a she-wolf?

- *Domande* Textbook p 87

- *Penna in mano! F Viva il calcio!* Workbook p 79

- *Studiamo la lingua! C Forza i verbi!* Workbook p 85

- *In poche parole 3A* Textbook p 88

This exercise provides a timely occasion to have another look at the map of Italy. Check again on the relative positions of **Roma**, **Firenze** and **Milano** and then take note of **Torino**, **Genova** and **Cagliari**. It would also be opportune to point out, without going fully into the regions of Italy, that **Lazio** is the name of the region in which Rome is situated.

The list of Italian teams in the *Textbook* is far from exhaustive. There could well be someone in the class who can provide you with more detailed information if anyone is so inclined. While you're on the subject of team colours, ask if anyone knows what the Italian team is called.

- *In poche parole 3B* Textbook p 88

- *Penna in mano! G Serie A* Workbook p 80

- *Su con l'orecchio! B Viva il calcio!* Workbook p 70, Cassette 4, tape script Teacher's Manual p 49

Once the basic exercise has been successfully completed by your class, return to the tape script and see if they can tell you:

1 What the interviewer first commented on.
2 Where the fan lives.
3 How **Lazio** is going.
4 Where **Cagliari** is.
5 What you call a **Juventus** fan. (Note that this fan is quoting from the doormat on page 89 of the *Textbook*.)
6 Who is playing in this derby.
7 Who is winning.
8 Why the interviewer is confused.

- *Rompicapi C I colori* Workbook p 88

- *Studiamo la lingua! D Che combinazione!* Workbook p 85

- *Studiamo la lingua! E Al dente!* Workbook p 86

- *Penna in mano! H Un weekend a Roma* Workbook p 80, repromaster Teacher's Manual p 52

STAGE 4

- *Lo Stadio dei Marmi* Textbook p 90

Lo Stadio dei Marmi is part of a complex of sporting facilities that includes **lo Stadio Olimpico**, **il Foro Italico** and the Roman tennis stadium, as well as the main swimming pool in the city.

Lo Stadio dei Marmi was built in the fascist era. Each Italian city was required to finance the sculpting of a marble statue for the stadium. The name of the provider-city is chiselled into the base of the statue. This stadium is the home of **la Scuola Giovanile di Atletica Leggera**, some members of which are seen practising here. The idea of providing aerobics for the waiting parents has proven to be very popular.

The four cities which are not mentioned in the text but visible at the base of the statues are **Arezzo**, **Cremona**, **Parma** and **Chieti**.

- *Domande* Textbook p 92

- *Penna in mano! I Lo Stadio dei Marmi* Workbook p 81

- *In poche parole 4A* Textbook p 92

- *In poche parole 4B* Textbook p 92

- *Penna in mano! J Marmi sportivi* Workbook p 82

- *Su con l'orecchio! C Parlano i marmi* Workbook p 71, Cassette 4, tape script Teacher's Manual p 50

- *Videogiochi* Textbook p 94

The items in this section are presented for reading enjoyment and, if desired, some free-flowing class discussion. The questions suggested here do not have the more formal status of the **Domande** of other sections but may provide the basis for some interesting conversation. You could initiate this with the class group as a whole and then allow students to continue their discussion in smaller groups or in pairs.

- *Su con l'orecchio! D Videogiochi* Workbook p 72, Cassette 4, tape script Teacher's Manual p 50

- *Su con l'orecchio! E Che tipo di persona è?* Workbook p 73, Cassette 4, tape script Teacher's Manual p 50

- *A lingua sciolta! 2 Test: Che tipo di persona sei?* Textbook p 96, repromaster Teacher's Manual p 53

- *Rompicapi D Cruciverba* Workbook p 89

Solution:

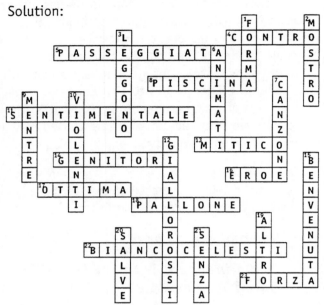

Suggested assessment tasks

Listening

- *Su con l'orecchio! A Non c'è niente da fare!* Workbook p 70, Cassette 4, tape script Teacher's Manual p 48

- *Su con l'orecchio! D Videogiochi* Workbook p 72, Cassette 4, tape script Teacher's Manual p 50

- *Su con l'orecchio! E Che tipo di persona è?* Workbook p 73, Cassette 4, tape script Teacher's Manual p 50

Speaking

- *In poche parole 1A and B* Textbook p 82

- *In poche parole 3A and B* Textbook p 88

- *A lingua sciolta! 1 La mia squadra preferita* Textbook p 89

- *A lingua sciolta! 2 Test: Che tipo di persona sei?* Textbook p 96, repromaster Teacher's Manual p 53

Reading

- *Penna in mano! A Non c'è niente da fare! I* Workbook p 74

- *Penna in mano! C Non c'è niente da fare! II* Workbook p 76

- *Penna in mano! I Lo Stadio dei Marmi* Workbook p 81

Writing

Penna in mano! B Chi sono e che cosa fanno? Workbook p 75

Penna in mano! E Parliamo di te! Workbook p 78

Penna in mano! J Marmi sportivi Workbook p 82

Penna in mano! K Una lettera a Nintendo Workbook p 83

Su con l'orecchio! Tape scripts

A Non c'è niente da fare!

Highlight the activity suggested to save each of these teenagers from boredom. Then highlight the activity they actually decide to do.

1 – Che noia! Non c'è niente da fare!
   – Ma Laura, perchè non ascolti un CD?
   – No, questi CD sono tutti noiosi. Vado al parco.
   – Che cosa fai lì?
   – Pattino.
   – Ma non ti piace pattinare da sola.
   – Non pattino da sola. Luisa è al parco oggi. Pattino con lei.

2 – Che c'è, Paolo? Stai male?
   – No, sto bene, ma non so che cosa fare!
   – Io faccio una passeggiata adesso. Perchè non vieni con me?
   – Una passeggiata?
   – Sì, vuoi venire?
   – No, non mi piace fare passeggiate.
   – Che cosa fai, allora? .
   – Gioco con un videogioco.
   – Che noia!

3 – Guardi la televisione? Tu guardi sempre la televisione! Basta per oggi!

– Che cosa fai, papà? Non c'è niente da fare adesso!

– Non dire stupidaggini! C'è molto da fare! Perchè non mi aiuti in cucina? Io preparo la cena.

– Ho un'idea! Mentre tu prepari la cena io suono la mia chitarra elettrica.

– Suoni la mia canzone preferita?

– Sì, suono la tua canzone preferita.

– Va bene.

4 – Non hai niente da fare?

– No, niente.

– Allora, vuoi fare il tuo letto?

– Sì, mamma, ma dopo.

– Dopo? Che cosa fai adesso?

– Faccio una passeggiata.

– Una passeggiata? Ma tu odi le passeggiate! Dove vai?

– No so. Ciao, mamma!

– E il tuo letto?

– Dopo, mamma, dopo.

5 – Come stai, Gina? Sana e allegra?

– Sana, sì, ma non molto allegra.

– Perchè no?

– Non ho niente da fare.

– Niente da fare? Non dire stupidaggini! Ecco un quaderno. Ecco una matita. Perchè non disegni?

– Che cosa?

– Non so. Una casa...

– Ma non voglio disegnare una casa. Non sono una bambina.

– Allora, che cosa vuoi fare?

– Niente. Io vado a fare i piatti.

– Tu fai i piatti? Poveretta, sei veramente ammalata!

– Spiritosa!

6 – Che cosa guardi?

– *I Simpsons*. È fantastico. È il mio programma preferito.

– Io vado al cinema. Vuoi venire?

– Che cosa vedi?

– *Il Re Leone*.

– No, grazie. Non mi piacciono i cartoni animati.

– Ma tu guardi...Va bene, che cosa fai dopo *I Simpsons*?

– Guardo un video.

– Un video? Che cos'è?

– *I Flintstones*.

– Uffa!

B Viva il calcio!

Which teams do these people support? Listen as these soccer fans are interviewed and then write the appropriate number in the column below.

1 – Scusa, dove vai adesso?

– Io? Vado all'Olimpico. C'è la partita oggi.

– Ma quella non è una sciarpa giallorossa.

– No, è viola. Io sono di Firenze.

– Ah, sei fiorentina.

– Sì. Sono fiorentina e tifo per la Fiorentina!

2 – Di dove sei?

– Sono di Roma.

– Ah, sei romano. Sei anche Romanista?

– No, sono Laziale.

– Come va la Lazio?

– Mmm, non c'è male.

3 – Sei tifosa?

– Sì, amo il calcio.

– Tifi per...?

– Il Cagliari. Tifo per il Cagliari. I rossoblù.

– Sei della Sardegna tu?

– Sì, sono della Sardegna.

4 – Juve! Juve!

– Scusa, che cosa fai?

– Guardo la partita...Oooo! Passa, passa! Tira! Oooo!

– Qual è la tua squadra?

– I bianconeri. Qui abita uno Juventino.

– Come vanno oggi?

– È zero a zero! Forza, Juve! Forza!

5 – Vado al cinema domenica sera. Vuoi venire?

– Domenica? Ma io vado alla partita.

– La partita?

– Sì, il derby: il Milan contro l'Inter.

– E tu tifi per chi?

– I nerazzurri.

– Il Milan?

– No.

– L'altra?

– Sì, l'altra. L'Inter.

6 – Io tifo per i rossoblù.

– Ah, sei sardo.

– Prego?

– Sei della Sardegna?

– Come?

– Non sei di Cagliari, in Sardegna?

– Io? No! Perchè?

– Tu tifi per i rossoblù.

– Sì, il Genoa. Sono di Genova.

– Ah, mi dispiace.

C Parlano i marmi

Which of the **marmi** is speaking? Write a number under the appropriate statue.

1 – Uffa, questo peso è veramente pesante.

2 – Mi piace boxare, ma non senza guanti. È troppo violento.

3 – Io sono alla piscina di Roma. Faccio il nuoto. Non nuoto molto bene perchè sono troppo pesante.

4 – Mi piace giocare a tennis, ma non mi piace giocare sempre nudo.

5 – Mi fanno male le mani perchè non ho guanti da boxe.

6 – Chi vuole giocare a pallone? Voi? Bene, ma state attenti, perchè questo pallone è pesantissimo. È di marmo.

D Videogiochi

Listen to these radio commercials for various video games and write a number under the appropriate graphic as you hear it being advertised.

1 – Vuoi giocare a pallone ma non ti piace andare in piazza? Vuoi tifare per una squadra ma non ti piace andare allo stadio? Vuoi essere un campione di calcio ma non ti piace andare fuori? Ecco il gioco per te.

2 – Benvenuti al mondo dell'avventura e della fantascienza! Tu sei l'eroe di una guerra intergalattica! Un'astronave da un altro mondo è all'attacco, ma tu non hai paura. Forza! L'umanità dipende da te. Un gioco tutto nuovo e divertente!

3 – Ti piacciono i giochi avventurosi ma non vuoi andare alla sala giochi? Non c'è problema. Adesso il super gorilla della giungla viene a giocare a casa tua. Tu hai paura del gorilla? Coraggio! Il gorilla ha paura di te.

4 – Non tutti i personaggi dei cartoni animati sono simpatici. In questo mondo abitano mostri terribili che vogliono mangiare ragazzi come Bart. Presto, vieni tu ad aiutare il tuo amico! Non sei bravo tu? Non sei forte? Un gioco di otto livelli divertenti.

5 – Aiuto! Ecco Gargamella, il mostro che vuole conquistare il mondo dei Puffi! Vuoi vincere la guerra contro Gargamella? Gioca tre livelli divertenti, con quattro livelli bonus.

E Che tipo di persona è?

Circle the answer this girl gives to each of the test questions and then work out which personality type she belongs to.

1 – Sei pronta per il test?

– Sì, sono pronta. Avanti!

– Va bene. Che cosa ti piace fare di più: ascoltare un CD, guardare la televisione, fare atletica o fare una passegiata con amici?

– Be', dipende. Mi piace ascoltare un CD mentre faccio una passeggiata con amici.

– Sì, ma che cosa ti piace fare di più, ascoltare o passeggiare?

– Ascoltare un CD.

– Brava! Grazie.

2 – Che cosa ti piace fare di più: suonare uno strumento musicale, giocare con un videogioco, nuotare in piscina o guardare i negozi in centro?

– Suonare uno strumento musicale.

– Che cosa suoni?

– La chitarra.

– Acustica o elettrica?

– Tutte e due. Ho una chitarra elettrica e una chitarra acustica.

3 – Che cosa ti piace fare di più: disegnare, giocare con internet, giocare a pallone in piazza o mangiare un gelato al parco?

– Mi piace disegnare ma amo internet. Sì, giocare con internet.

4 – Che cosa ti piace fare di più: cantare alla sala karaoke, andare alla sala giochi, andare in bicicletta, o andare da amici?
– Andare in bicicletta alla sala giochi.
– Spiritosa! Che cosa ti piace di più, la bicicletta o la sala giochi?
– La sala giochi.
– Grazie.
– Prego.

5 – Che cosa ti piace fare di più: fare fotografie, guardare un video, pattinare o andare al cinema?
– Mi piace fare fotografie.
– Fare fotografie?!
– Sì, è il mio hobby. Faccio le foto a casa, a scuola, in città…ho la mia macchina fotografica sempre con me.
– Vuoi fare una fotografia a me?
– Mi dispiace, non ho un rullino adesso. Senti, che tipo di persona sono?
– Mmm, vediamo un po'…

Un weekend a Roma

Cari signori,

Mi piace Roma perchè è molto bella e molto interessante. Voglio fare un giro di Roma antica. Voglio vedere le piazze, le fontane, i palazzi e i monumenti di Roma.

Voglio vedere il Colosseo. Ha quasi duemila anni ed è bellissimo. Non voglio vedere i gatti lì perchè non mi piacciono i gatti.

Voglio andare al Foro Romano, il centro di Roma antica. Voglio parlare latino con gli antichi romani.

Mi dispiace, ma non mi piace il monumento a Vittorio Emanuele. Non è brutto, ma è troppo grande e troppo bianco!!!

Voglio guardare una partita di calcio all'Olimpico. Io tifo per la Roma. Sono romanista perchè mi piacciono i colori giallo e rosso. Voglio comprare una sciarpa giallorossa e gridare Forza Roma!

Grazie.

Travis Stevens.

TEST: Che tipo di persona sei?

test

Che cosa ti piace fare di più?

1
- a ☐ ascoltare un CD
- b ☐ guardare la televisione
- c ☐ fare atletica
- d ☐ fare una passeggiata con amici

2
- a ☐ suonare uno strumento musicale
- b ☐ giocare con un videogioco
- c ☐ nuotare in piscina
- d ☐ guardare i negozi in centro

3
- a ☐ disegnare
- b ☐ giocare con l'internet
- c ☐ giocare a pallone in piazza
- d ☐ mangiare un gelato al parco

4
- a ☐ cantare alla sala karaoke
- b ☐ andare alla sala giochi
- c ☐ andare in bicicletta
- d ☐ andare da amici

5
- a ☐ fare fotografie
- b ☐ guardare un video
- c ☐ pattinare
- d ☐ andare al cinema

Mi piace nuotare in piscina.

NUOTA CON TE

- **a** *Sei una persona artistica e creativa.*
- **b** *Sei una persona moderna, computerizzata e teledipendente.*
- **c** *Sei una persona sportiva e in forma.*
- **d** *Sei una persona simpatica e hai molti amici.*

Forza! uno student progress sheet

In the **io** column, give yourself a tick for each thing that you know how to do in Italian. Then ask a friend to check you and mark the **amico/a** column. Keep the last column free for when your teacher has time to hear how you are progressing.

Nome _____ **Classe** _____

Capitolo 5	io	amico/a	
Complain that there is nothing to do			
Suggest various things to do			
Suggest various places to go			
Ask people what they want to do			
Say what you want to do			
Say what you like doing			
Ask people what they like doing most			
Say what you like doing most			
Say you think something is boring			
Ask people to go to the movies			
Talk about different types of movies			
Talk about singing and playing music			
Talk about soccer in Italy			
Talk about team colours			
Say which team you support			
Talk about your favourite players			
Talk about other sports			
Ask people where they are from			
Say where you are from			
Talk about video games			

Suggested procedure

STAGE 1

• *Preparatory activity*

Introduce the topic **I mezzi di trasporto**, by talking to your students about travelling to school and listing key words on the board: **Io vado a scuola con la macchina. Mi piace la mia macchina: è una Toyota rossa. È piccola, ma è veloce! E voi, come andate a scuola? Come vai a scuola, Rosie? Con l'autobus? Con il tram? Chi va a scuola a piedi? E tu prendi il treno, non è vero? Ah, anche tu vai con la macchina. Chi va in bicicletta? Porti un casco? Chi usa due (tre, quattro) mezzi di trasporto?**

• *In giro a Roma* Textbook p 98

Listen to and read this photo-presentation.

You could begin by reminding the class that motor vehicles in Italy are left-hand drive and that traffic travels on the right-hand side of the road. This is particularly relevant to pedestrians: you have to go against years of habit and remember to look to the left before you cross the road. It is surprising how hard this can be!

Looking at frame 1 you could ask:

1 **Che cosa porta l'uomo che pattina? (Un casco, uno zaino)**

2 **Di che colore è la macchina?**

3 **Qual è il numero dell'autobus?**

Note the sign on the bus saying **ENTRATA**.

Note in frame 2, in the background, a section of the wall that enclosed the ancient city of Rome.

In frame 3, the girl wearing the helmet is the one who is breaking the law. On the small **motorini** (less than 125 cc) you don't have to wear a helmet, but you are not allowed to carry a passenger.

The little boy in frame 4 is riding his bike in **Piazza Navona**.

In frame 5, this **carrozza** is one of a number parked outside **il Colosseo**, offering tours of ancient Rome. In the background is **l'Arco di Costantino** and the lower slopes of **il Palatino**. **Il Foro Romano** is to the right.

In frame 6, the **carabinieri** are riding around **Piazza Navona**. You could explain that **i carabinieri** are part of the Italian army and form the most prestigious, and glamorous, police force in the country. Later the class will meet **un vigile**, a member of the local police force assigned to less exciting aspects of police work such as traffic duty.

Regarding frame 7, you could mention that pedestrian crossings in Italy do not have the same protective power as they do in some other countries. You certainly would not step out onto a crossing and assume that the traffic will stop for you! This one is all right; it has traffic lights and pedestrian signals. Ask your students to read what the signal says now. Point out that when it is red it says **ALT**.

Frame 8 is actually the beginning of a story that is taken up later in the chapter. Notice that the important verb **prendere** is introduced here. Explain to the class that it has the general meaning of 'to take' but that sometimes we would use other English equivalents that vary according to the context. Ask what meaning your class would give to the verb in the two examples given here.

Two other important language points are introduced here: **potere** and **dovere**. They will be followed up throughout the chapter. For the time being it is enough for your students to understand what is being said here.

You could also mention that **capo** is a form of address used by some people in Rome in much the same way as people elsewhere might say 'chief', 'guv' or even 'mate'. Here Antonio probably means to say 'boss'.

• *In poche parole 1A* Textbook p 101

• *Penna in mano! A In giro a Roma* Workbook p 95

• *In poche parole 1B* Textbook p 101

• *Su con l'orecchio! A Come vanno a scuola?* Workbook p 90, Cassette 4, tape script Teacher's Manual p 61

As in previous chapters, return to the tape script once the basic exercise has been successfully completed by your class. See if they can tell you:

1 What extra information this person gives about travelling to school.

2 Why this person sounds a bit flustered.

3 Why the interviewer probably ended up smiling.

4 Why this person is happy about travelling to school by bus.

5 Why the interviewer was so impressed with this person.

6 Why the interviewer ended up a bit frustrated.

- *Rompicapi A Troviamo le parole!* *Workbook p 110*

Solution: 1 **Piazza della Repubblica** 2 **Castel Sant'Angelo** 3 **Piazza del Popolo** 4 **il Foro Romano** 5 **il Colosseo** 6 **Stazione Termini** 7 **Fontana di Trevi** 8 **Piazza San Pietro** 9 **Piazza Venezia**

You must do **un giro a Roma** to see all the sights.

- *Rompicapi D Mezzi di trasporto* *Workbook p 112*

Solution: 1 **macchina** 2 **cavallo** 3 **bicicletta** 4 **tram** 5 **carrozza** 6 **autobus** 7 **taxi** 8 **aereo** 9 **motorino** 10 **piede** 11 **mezzi di trasporto** 12 **treno** 13 **pattini**

- *A tu per tu 1* *Textbook p 102*

This exercise provides some simple practice with parts of **dovere** and **potere**, specifically **devo**, **posso** and **puoi**. You could show how **devo** and **posso** work with an infinitive in much the same way as **voglio**.

You could tell your students about the chaotic parking conditions that prevail in Rome, to the extent that footpath space is often stolen by cars cramming into every available centimetre. This altercation is taking place in **Via della Conciliazione**, the broad avenue leading to **San Pietro** (more about this later in the chapter). Your students will probably remember the signs telling dogs to wait outside. **Dogpark** offers the marvellous facility of a hook to tie your leash to. It should not be used for troublesome children.

STAGE 2

- *Antonio ha fretta* *Textbook p 103*

The opening sentence reminds the reader that Antonio has answered a radio call to pick up a woman at the Trevi Fountain. Can your students remember the answer to this question: **Perchè la donna alla Fontana di Trevi è in fretta?**

You could tell your students that **Piazza Venezia** is one of the busiest squares in Rome. Traffic converges on it from all directions and it is left to a lone **vigile** to untangle it. **Il monumento a Vittorio Emanuele** is on this **piazza** and many of the other monuments (e.g. **il Foro Romano, il Colosseo**) are nearby.

Antonio certainly isn't taking a short-cut by going to the Trevi Fountain from **Piazza Venezia** via **Piazza Bologna**. But how else would we get to see **i vigili del fuoco**?

Your students need to understand that **la Fontana di Trevi** is one of the major tourist attractions in Rome. Have they heard of the custom of throwing in coins for the guarantee of a return to the Eternal City? (And the custom, observed by some of the local youngsters, of diving for the coins?)

- *Penna in mano! C Vero o falso?* *Workbook p 96*

- *Perchè? Perchè? Perchè?* *Textbook p 105*

Treat this as an oral exercise first, taking the opportunity to revise the story and iron out comprehension problems.

- *Penna in mano! D Perchè? Perchè? Perchè?* *Workbook p 97*

- *In poche parole 2A* *Textbook p 106*

Before tackling the next two exercises, it may be worthwhile to revisit **Un giro di Roma** in **Capitolo 4**, for it was here that your students first read and heard about **il Colosseo**, **il Foro Romano** and **il Castel Sant'Angelo**. This was also the chapter in which they learned the expressions **a destra** and **a sinistra**.

The new expression **diritto** is introduced in frames 2 and 3 of the **fotoromanzo** entitled **Antonio ha fretta**. **Piazza del Popolo** is not mentioned anywhere, but you can tell your class the man on the in-line skates early in this chapter was photographed there. **San Pietro** has been glimpsed in **Capitolo 1** and will be visited more thoroughly later in this chapter, as will **Stazione Termini**, the main railway station in Rome.

To help set the scene for this exercise, ask your class to imagine they are driving around Rome with a friend; one of them is at the wheel, the other has the map.

For the purposes of both exercises, they are in **Piazza Venezia**. In exercise A they are facing north (along **Via del Corso**) towards **Piazza del Popolo**. In exercise B they are facing (roughly) east towards **Stazione Termini**. They can use the map of Rome on page 185 of the *Textbook* to help orient themselves better.

People in Italy vary in their use of articulated prepositions with well-known places about town: for example, they might say **a** (rather than **alla**) **Stazione Termini**. For the sake of consistency, it is probably better to practise them all with the article (except, of course, **San Pietro**).

- *In poche parole 2B* Textbook p 106

- *Penna in mano! E In Piazza Venezia* Workbook p 98

- *Su con l'orecchio! B Dove vanno?* Workbook p 90, Cassette 4, tape script Teacher's Manual p 61

- *Antonio ha fretta* Textbook p 103
Listen to and read this **fotoromanzo** again.

STAGE 3

- *Preparatory activity*

Introduce the topic of **Il Vaticano** by finding out how much your students already know about it:

1 **Dov'è il Vaticano?**
2 **Chi abita nel Vaticano?**
3 **Come si chiama il capo della Chiesa Cattolica?** (You will need to provide **il Papa**, distinguishing it from **il papà** of Capitolo 3.)
4 **Come si chiama il Papa?**
5 **Come si chiama la grande chiesa nel Vaticano?**

You could point out that the Vatican, although situated in Rome, is actually an independent state, with its own government and a separate vote in the United Nations. Other countries appoint ambassadors to the Vatican as well as to Italy. If you touched on **il Risorgimento** in connection with **Vittorio Emanuele in Capitolo 4**, your class might remember that the Papal States were a major political force before the unification of Italy. This tiny enclave in Rome is all that remains. Perhaps the most easily identifiable sign of the separateness of the Vatican is the post office in **Piazza San Pietro** selling Vatican stamps (see page 160).

- *Guardiamo il Vaticano* Textbook p 107
Listen to and read this **fotoromanzo**.

Obviously, there is a wealth of historical and cultural detail available on this topic and you might encourage some of your students to explore it further. Everyone will be interested to know that **San Pietro** is the biggest church in the world and that there are marks on the floor inside to show where other big churches come to. It is 200 metres long, 130 metres wide and can hold 60 000 people. **Figuratevi!** Building of the present basilica (a more humble mounument existed on the site of St Peter's grave for over 1000 years) was begun in 1506 and took over 150 years to complete.

The Sistine Chapel is a nondescript building to the right of St Peter's in frame 3. It is here that the cardinals of the world congregate to elect a new pope, sending a puff of white smoke from the chimney to announce that the election has been successfully completed. It is most famous, of course, for the frescoes of Michelangelo, who spent untold hours in excruciating discomfort on scaffolding, painting the ceiling of the chapel. The frescoes have been recently restored. The text of the **fotoromanzo** makes the point that you are not allowed to speak in the chapel but this directive is sytematically ignored by most visitors despite the constant annoucements and remonstrations of the patrolling attendants.

Michelangelo was also responsible for the beautiful **cupola di San Pietro** which soars to a height of 119 metres. In the view presented in the *Textbook*, your students should be able to recognise **il Castel Sant'Angelo** and accept that the line of trees they see marks the course of **il Tevere**. The street leading into the square is **Via della Conciliazione**, in which the woman was having parking problems earlier in the chapter.

The monk who is complaining about not being allowed into **San Pietro** is probably fibbing a little, but he does make the point about the dress code enforced by the Vatican attendants at the entrance to the basilica. Sandals, short skirts, sleeveless and low-cut tops are all on the not-acceptable list, much to the chagrin of many a tourist dressing light to cope with the hot Roman summer. (One person the attendants did let in some years ago was the Australian citizen who took to Michelangelo's **Pietà** with a hammer.)

The large crowd assembled in the square, including a substantial military component, is awaiting the Pope's Christmas blessing. The Pope impressed this crowd with his ability to deliver the blessing in twenty languages. The weekly papal blessing is not usually delivered from this balcony at the front of the basilica, but from a window (top floor, second from the right) of his apartment.

- *Domande* Textbook p 109

- *Penna in mano! F Guardiamo il Vaticano* Workbook p 99

- *A tu per tu 2* Textbook p 110
This exercise is slightly different in format from most others under this heading, but the procedure is much the same. Begin by modelling the question/answer pattern with some of your students and then ask them to work in pairs. Encourage them to muster the appropriate tone of disdain for the dismissive **non è un gran che**, 'it's no big deal', 'it's nothing to write home about'.

- *A tu per tu 3* Textbook p 110
This is another variation on the **A tu per tu** theme. 'A' plays the role of the tourist while 'B' takes the part of the Swiss Guard. The answers to some of the questions are in the text of the **fotoromanzo**, others can be based on common sense.

- *Penna in mano! G Fotografie del Vaticano* Workbook p 100

- *Su con l'orecchio! D La Guardia Svizzera* Workbook p 92, Cassette 4, tape script Teacher's Manual p 62
Return to the tape script once the basic exercise has been successfully completed by your class. See if they can tell you:
1   What the woman asked the Guard after he told her where the basilica is.
2   How the woman was advised to look for St Peter's dome.
3   What the Guard thought of the man who asked about St Peter's Square.
4   The mistake made by the person looking for the Sistine Chapel.
5   What the person looking for the papal apartment wanted to do.

- *Penna in mano! O Venite al Vaticano!* Workbook p 107

- *Su con l'orecchio! C Un lavoro difficile!* Workbook p 91, Cassette 4, tape script Teacher's Manual p 62
Return to the tape script once the basic exercise has been successfully completed by your class. See if they answer the following questions:
1   What alternative does the **vigile** offer the person swimming in the fountain?
2   How does the motorist argue the case to be allowed to park?
3   What helpful advice does the **vigile** give the kids playing **pallone**?
4   What reason does the motorist give for wanting to turn?
5   Does the **vigile** book the people riding the scooter in the square?
6   Does the person eating on the steps feel very guilty about it?

- *Studiamo la lingua! A Volere, potere, dovere I* Workbook p 108

- *Studiamo la lingua! B Volere, potere, dovere II* Workbook p 108

- *Studiamo la lingua! C Nella bella cappella I* Workbook p 108

- *Studiamo la lingua! D Nella bella cappella II* Workbook p 109

- **Su con l'orecchio! G La dolce vita**
  Workbook p 94, Cassette 4, tape script
  Teacher's Manual p 64

This listening exercise serves as a useful preparation for the **A lingua sciolta!** activity to follow. Once the class has attempted to fill-in the survey sheet for Giorgia, play the tape through again, stopping it after she has answered each question. See if your students can give you some of the detail in her responses.

- **A lingua sciolta! La dolce vita**
  Textbook p 117, repromaster
  Teacher's Manual p 66

STAGE 4

- **Guardie in vacanze** Textbook p 113

The holiday season was announced in the previous **fotoromanzo** which featured a Christmas tree in **Piazza San Pietro**. Even slightly silly Swiss Guards would not consider taking a tourist carriage from **San Pietro** to **Stazione Termini**. Students can (roughly) follow the route of the 64 bus on the map on page 106 or on the **Pianta di Roma** at the back of the *Textbook*.

The **Pendolino** is the showpiece of the **Ferrovie dello Stato** (**FS**). While not achieving the speeds of the TGV in France or even the Shinkansen in Japan, it is very fast, cutting hours off long train trips such as Rome–Venice and Rome–Milan. Its nickname comes from its habit of swaying or leaning as it rounds bends in the track at full speed. If you want to travel on this special train you have to book a seat.

The (relatively) new train that connects **Termini** with the airport at **Fiumicino** is a much more efficient means of transport than the buses which most travellers had to take. Notice that you have to punch the ticket in a machine to validate it before setting foot on the train. Some people have been known to get into trouble for failing to do just that!

Some maps appear to show Rome on the west coast of Italy, but it is actually about 30 kilometres inland. **Fiumicino** is very close to the coastline and the beach town of **Ostia** is nearby.

- **Penna in mano! K Guardie in vacanze I** Workbook p 104

- **Domande** Textbook p 116

Questions 11 and 12 afford an opportunity to practise with different departure times and platform numbers. All you have to do is vary the time at the start.

You will need to establish that the train only operates from 7 a.m. to 9.15 p.m., so that when you say **sono le tre** you mean it's 3 p.m. The times on the **Partenze** board follow the 24-hour clock, so that when you say **sono le quattro** students will need to look for the next train after **le sedici**. There is a reprise of this sort of exercise on page 120.

- **Su con l'orecchio! F Il prossimo treno**
  Workbook p 93, Cassette 4, tape script
  Teacher's Manual p 63

- **Penna in mano! L Guardie in vacanze II** Workbook p 105

- **In poche parole 3A** Textbook p 119

With the Swiss Guards heading back to Bern for the Christmas holidays it is time to give your students a glimpse of Italy in its wider European context. For the purposes of the oral exercise it was necessary to select a limited number of cities and countries. If there are students from other European countries in your class you might consider having students mark them in, with their capitals, on the map in the *Workbook*. You could then include them in the exercise.

Before tackling the **In poche parole** dialogues it would be a good idea to practise saying the names of the cities and the countries on the map. Does your class remember how to say 'Scarno lives in Rome', 'I live *in* Richmond' etc? You can go on to point out that **a** also means 'to' when used with cities. Contrast this with **in** meaning 'in' and 'to' with (most) countries.

- **In poche parole 3B** Textbook p 119

- **Penna in mano! M Europa**
  Workbook p 106

- **Studiamo la lingua! E Dove vai?**
  Workbook p 109

- **Studiamo la lingua! F I verbi -ire**
  Workbook p 109

- *Studiamo la lingua! G Partite per la partita?* Workbook p 110

- *Su con l'orecchio! E Dove vanno per le vacanze?* Textbook p 93, Cassette 4, tape script Teacher's Manual p 63

Return to the tape script once the basic exercise has been successfully completed by your class. See if they can answer the following questions:

1 What advantage does this person have?
2 When is this person leaving for Greece?
3 Who is this person going to visit for Christmas? In which city?
4 What city did this person think was the capital of Switzerland? What is Bern like?
5 How is this person preparing for their holiday in France?
6 Does this person speak much Spanish?

- *In poche parole 4A* Textbook p 120

- *In poche parole 4B* Textbook p 120

- *Penna in mano! N All'aeroporto* Workbook p 107

- *Rompicapi C No, non qui!* Workbook p 111

- *Rompicapi E Cruciverba* Workbook p 113
Solution:

Suggested assessment tasks

Listening

- *Su con l'orecchio! A Come vanno a scuola?* Workbook p 90, Cassette 4, tape script Teacher's Manual p 61

- *Su con l'orecchio! B Dove vanno?* Workbook p 90, Cassette 4, tape script Teacher's Manual p 61

- *Su con l'orecchio! F Il prossimo treno* Workbook p 93, Cassette 4, tape script Teacher's Manual p 63

- *Su con l'orecchio! G La dolce vita* Workbook p 94, Cassette 4, tape script Teacher's Manual p 64

Speaking

- *In poche parole 1A* Textbook p 101
- *A tu per tu 1* Textbook p 102
- *In poche parole 2A or B* Textbook p 106
- *A tu per tu 3* Textbook p 110
- *A lingua sciolta! La dolce vita* Textbook p 117, repromaster Teacher's Manual p 66
- *In poche parole 3A* Textbook p 119

Reading

- *Penna in mano! C Vero o falso?* Workbook p 96
- *Penna in mano! D Perchè? Perchè? Perchè?* Workbook p 97
- *Penna in mano! F Guardiamo il Vaticano* Workbook p 99

Writing

Penna in mano! B E tu, come vai? Workbook p 96

Penna in mano! E In Piazza Venezia Workbook p 98

Penna in mano! G Fotografie del Vaticano Workbook p 100

Penna in mano! I Mi dispiace, non posso Workbook p 102

Penna in mano! N All'aeroporto Workbook p 107

Su con l'orecchio!
Tape scripts

A Come vanno a scuola?

How do these people get to school? Highlight the means of transport they use.

1 – Scusa, posso fare una domanda?

   – Sì, prego.

   – Come vai a scuola?

   – Io? Io vado con la macchina.

   – La macchina di tuo padre?

   – Di mia madre. E passiamo a prendere la mia amica Silvia.

   – Bene. Grazie.

   – Prego.

2 – Aspetti un tram?

   – Sì, aspetto un tram. Che ore sono, per favore?

   – Sono le otto meno cinque.

   – Accidenti! Sono in ritardo.

   – Vai a scuola con il tram?

   – Sì. Ah, ecco, arriva adesso.

   – Grazie. Arrivederci.

3 – Scusa, posso fare una domanda?

   – Mi dispiace, non ho tempo. Ho fretta.

   – Dove vai?

   – A scuola.

   – Vai così, a piedi?

   – Sì, vado a piedi.

   – Grazie.

4 – E tu, come vai a scuola?

   – Prendo l'autobus.

   – Il numero 70?

   – No, prendo il numero 72.

   – Ti piace andare con l'autobus?

   – Non c'è male. Posso leggere un libro. E qualche volta faccio i compiti.

   – Fai i compiti nell'autobus?

   – Qualche volta, sì.

5 – Quale mezzo di trasporto usi per andare a scuola?

   – Io uso questo qui.

   – La bicicletta?

   – La bicicletta.

   – Quanti chilometri ci sono da casa tua a scuola?

   – Dodici.

   – Mamma mia, sei veramente in forma!

6 – Anche tu vai con la bicicletta?

   – Io? No. Io vado con il motorino.

   – Con il motorino? Quanti anni hai tu?

   – Ho quattordici, quasi quindici anni.

   – E tu hai un motorino?

   – È di mio fratello. Ma adesso lui ha una macchina ed io vado con il suo motorino.

   – Porti un casco?

   – Qualche volta. Scusa, devo andare adesso. Ciao!

   – Ciao!

B Dove vanno?

Write a number on the appropriate part of the map to show that you understand where each of these people is heading. Then, for each number below the map, highlight the direction they take to get there.

1 – Un momento, dove vai?

   – Vogliamo andare alla stazione, no?

   – Alla Stazione Termini?

   – Sì.

   – Per la Stazione Termini dobbiamo girare a destra.

   – Non posso andare diritto?

   – No, devi girare a destra.

   – Va bene, giro a destra qui. Sei contento adesso?

   – Sì.

2 – Vado bene per il Colosseo?

   – Vediamo un po'. No, per il Colosseo dobbiamo andare a sinistra.

   – Va bene, giro qui.

   – No, non puoi girare qui. È vietato. Prendi la prossima strada...Sì, qui. Vedi? Il Colosseo, a sinistra.

   – Brava, sei veramente brava.

3 – Dove siamo adesso?

   – Non so, è una grande piazza. Ah, ecco il nome. Si chiama Piazza del Popolo.

   – È bella. E adesso, come andiamo a Piazza Venezia?

– Diritto. Sempre diritto.

– Non devo girare?

– No. Se vuoi andare a Piazza Venezia, vai diritto.

4 – Possiamo prendere questa strada per San Pietro?

– Non so. Aspetta che guardo un po'...No, per San Pietro dobbiamo girare a destra.

– A destra? Dove?

– Alla prossima strada.

– Va bene...questa è la prossima strada...

– No, non qui. Al prossimo semaforo.

– Uffa!

5 – Dove vuoi andare adesso?

– Alla Fontana di Trevi.

– Un'altra fontana! Sono stufo di fontane!

– Dobbiamo vedere la Fontana di Trevi! Non possiamo venire a Roma senza vedere la Fontana di Trevi.

– Va bene, va bene. È diritto, no?

– Sì.

6 – Ah finalmente, il Tevere. Il Castel Sant'Angelo è a sinistra o a destra?

– A sinistra.

– Va bene, giro qui a sinistra.

– Perchè non parcheggiamo qui? Non si può mai parcheggiare a Castel Sant'Angelo. Possiamo andare a piedi.

– Va bene.

C Un lavoro difficile

Vigili in Rome spend much of their time stopping people doing things they are not allowed to do. Write a number under the appropriate illustration below to show that you understand which **vigile** is speaking.

1 – Fuori, per favore!

– Come?

– Fuori! Non si può nuotare qui!

– Ma...

– È una fontana. Se vuoi nuotare, vai in piscina!

2 – Ma signore, non si può!

– Come?

– Non si può. È vietato parcheggiare qui.

– Ma non ci sono posti. È solo per cinque minuti.

– No, mi dispiace, non si può parcheggiare qui.

– Accidenti!

3 – Ehi, ragazzi, non potete giocare qui.

– Dove possiamo giocare, allora?

– Non lo so, ma qui è vietato. Perchè non andate al parco?

– Ma non si può giocare al pallone nel parco.

– Lo so, ma non ci sono vigili nel parco oggi.

– Grazie.

– Arrivederci.

– Ciao, ragazzi.

4 – ...ma devo andare alla stazione.

– Mi dispiace, signore, ma non si può girare qui.

– Ma devo...

– No, qui è vietato. Deve andare diritto.

5 – Ma dove andate voi?

– Andiamo lì.

– In motorino, no. Scendete, per favore. Dovete andare a piedi. È vietato andare in motorino qui in piazza. Sì?

– Va bene.

6 – No, non si può!

– Non ci credo! Non posso mangiare? Ho fame!

– Ma qui non si può! È vietato.

D La Guardia Svizzera

They are not really supposed to, but tourists are always asking the Swiss Guards the way around the Vatican. Write the appropriate number next to whatever the people are asking about.

1 – Scusi, voglio vedere San Pietro.

– Prego, signora?

– San Pietro, la basilica di San Pietro.

– È questa grande chiesa qui, signora.

– Grazie. La mia amica può fare una fotografia a noi due?

2 – Scusi. Il Papa abita qui nel Vaticano, vero?

– Sì, signore. Abita lì, in quel palazzo.

– In quel palazzo lì?

– Sì, l'appartamento del Papa è in quel palazzo.

– Voglio parlare con il Papa. Posso andare al suo appartamento?

– No, signore. È vietato. Mi dispiace.

3 – Scusi, dov'è la cupola di San Pietro?

– La cupola? Guardi in su, signora.

– È quella? Mamma mia, è grandissima!

– Sì, signora. Arrivederci, signora.

4 – Scusi, dov'è Piazza San Pietro?

– È qui, signore. Questa è Piazza San Pietro.

– Aahh, questa è Piazza San Pietro. Grazie.

– Prego. Cretino!

5 – È questa la Cappella Sistina?

– No, signora, questa è la basilica di San Pietro.

– Dov'è la Cappella Sistina, allora?

– È lì, signora.

– Grazie. Arrivederci.

E Dove vanno per le vacanze?

In which countries will these people be spending their Christmas holidays? For each person, write the appropriate number on the map below.

1 – Dove vai per le vacanze di Natale?

– Vado in Inghilterra.

– Ah, ma sei fortunata! Parli inglese?

– Un po'.

– Brava! Buona vacanza, allora.

– Grazie.

2 – Quando parti?

– Il 22 dicembre.

– E vai direttamente ad Atene?

– Sì.

– Che bello! Amo la Grecia.

– Anch'io.

3 – Passi il Natale in Germania?!

– Sì, ho un cugino lì.

– Che bello! A Berlino?

– No, a Francoforte.

– Com'è Francoforte? È una bella città?

– Be', non lo so.

4 – ...e arrivo a Ginevra il 24.

– Benissimo! Ginevra è la capitale della Svizzera, vero?

– No, la capitale è Berna.

– Vero? È una grande città, allora?

– Non molto grande. Ma è bella.

– Buon viaggio, allora.

– Grazie. Arrivederci.

5 – *Au revoir!*

– Come?

– È francese per 'arrivederci'. Io parto per la Francia domani.

– Vai in Francia! Che bello! Dove vai – a Parigi?

– A Parigi, sì.

– Allora – come si dice? – *au revoir!*

– Ciao!

6 – Vai via per le vacanze o rimani qui a Roma?

– Vado via.

– Ah sì? Dove?

– In Spagna. Ci credi?

– Fantastico! Parli spagnolo?

– Un po'. *Ole!*

– *Ole!*

F Il prossimo treno

Next to each city on the map below write the time of the next train that goes there and the platform it leaves from.

1 – Buonasera.

– Buonasera.

– A che ora parte il prossimo treno per Firenze?

– Per Firenze? Un momento. Parte alle sedici e trenta.

– Alle sedici e trenta? Grazie. E da che binario?

– Dal binario quindici.

– Grazie.

– Prego.

2 – Scusi, c'è un treno per Genova stasera?

– Ci sono due treni per Genova stasera.

– Va bene. A che ora parte il prossimo treno?

– Il prossimo treno per Genova parte alle diciassette e cinque.

– Da questo binario?

– No, dal binario ùndici. È lì in fondo.

3 – Scusi, ho fretta! Dov'è il binario numero quattro?

– Numero quattro? Il treno per Roma?

– Sì, sì.

– È lì in fondo, ma non c'è fretta. Il treno per Roma è in ritardo. Parte alle quindici e quaranta.

– Alle quindici e *quaranta!* Ho venti minuti, allora. Grazie.

– Prego.

4 – Scusi, voglio prendere il prossimo treno per Napoli.

– Il prossimo treno per Napoli parte alle diciannove e trenta.

– Alle sette e mezza. Va bene. Binario otto?

– Binario otto, sì.

5 – Devo andare a Palermo stasera. C'è un treno verso le dieci?

– C'è un treno alle ventuno e cinquanta.

– Mmm, le dieci meno dieci. È il prossimo?

– Sì, signora.

– Va bene. E da che binario parte?

– Parte dal binario diciotto.

6 – A che ora parte il prossimo treno per Milano?

– Il prossimo treno per Milano è il Pendolino. Parte alle ventitré e dieci.

– Va bene. Da che binario?

– Dal binario numero uno.

– Benissimo. Due biglietti per favore.

– Mi dispiace, non ci sono posti. È Natale, ragazzi, dovete prenotare!

G La dolce vita

Listen as Giorgia is interviewed about her life and see if she leads **la dolce vita** or not. Fill in the survey sheet and add up her points. How does she compare with people in your class?

– Ciao, Giorgia. Devo fare queste domande. Puoi rispondere?

– Sì, come no? Avanti!

– Allora, puoi guardare la televisione mentre mangi?

– No, non posso. A casa dobbiamo parlare mentre mangiamo.

– Con chi devi parlare?

– Con tutti: con mamma, con papà, con mio fratello, con mia sorella – con la famiglia, insomma.

– Secondo me è una buon'idea. Va bene, la seconda domanda. Puoi mangiare fast-food?

– Mmm, qualche volta. Domenica sera mamma e papà non vogliono preparare la cena, allora qualche volta mangiamo un hamburger o una pizza.

– Tre punti, allora. E puoi guardare i film per adulti?

– A casa o al cinema?

– A casa.

– Mmm, dipende. Qualche volta, sì.

– E puoi andare in città con amici?

– Sì, come no?

– Sempre?

– Sì, ma devo tornare alle dieci.

– Mmm, va bene. Puoi andare alla sala giochi?

– No, alla sala giochi, no. Quando ho sedici anni sì, ma adesso no.

– Mai?

– Mai.

– Puoi invitare gli amici a casa?

– Qualche volta, sì. Vuoi venire da me?

– Ah, non so. Ma prima devo finire queste domande. Puoi dormire a casa di amici?

– Sì.

– Sempre?

– Sì.

– Puoi ascoltare la musica mentre fai i compiti?

– No, da me è vietato. Dobbiamo fare i compiti in silenzio.

– E le riviste?

– Come?

– Le riviste. Puoi leggere le riviste che ti piacciono?

– No. A casa no.

– Dal dentista?

– Il mio dentista non ha le riviste che mi piacciono. Qualche volta dalla mia amica.

– Lei può comprare le riviste che ti piacciono?

– Sì.

– Adesso parliamo delle cose che devi fare.

– Va bene.

– Devi fare i piatti?

– Sì. Tocca a me domenica e giovedì.

– Mmm, qualche volta allora. Sono tre punti. E devi fare i compiti?

– Sì, sempre. E in silenzio.

– Devi fare il tuo letto?

– Sì, ogni giorno.

– Sempre?

– Sempre.

– Devi fare la spesa?

– No. Papà fa la spesa.

– E tu mai?

– Mai.

– E devi lavorare in giardino?

– No, mai.

– Ti piace lavorare in giardino?

– No.

– Va bene. Grazie. È finito.

– Finito?

– Sì.

– Com'è la mia vita allora? Ho la vita facile?
La dolce vita?

– Mmm. Vediamo un po...

Capitolo 6

La dolce vita

Nome_____ **Classe**_____

Puoi...

	sempre 5 punti	qualche volta 3 punti	mai 0 punti
guardare la televisione mentre mangi?	❑	❑	❑
mangiare fast-food?	❑	❑	❑
guardare i film per adulti?	❑	❑	❑
andare in città con gli amici?	❑	❑	❑
andare alla sala giochi?	❑	❑	❑
invitare a casa gli amici?	❑	❑	❑
dormire a casa di amici?	❑	❑	❑
ascoltare la musica mentre fai i compiti?	❑	❑	❑
leggere le riviste che ti piacciono?	❑	❑	❑

Devi...

	mai 5 punti	qualche volta 3 punti	sempre 0 punti
fare i piatti?	❑	❑	❑
fare i compiti?	❑	❑	❑
fare il tuo letto?	❑	❑	❑
fare la spesa?	❑	❑	❑
lavorare in giardino?	❑	❑	❑

Forza! uno student progress sheet

In the **io** column, give yourself a tick for each thing that you know how to do in Italian. Then ask a friend to check you and mark the **amico/a** column. Keep the last column free for when your teacher has time to hear how you are progressing.

Nome _____ **Classe** _____

Capitolo 6	io	amico/a	
Say how people get around town			
Say how you like to get around			
Say where you have to go			
Say what you have to do			
Ask someone if they can do something			
Say what you can and can't do			
Say that something can be done			
Say that something is not allowed			
Say that of course it's all right			
Say that something is no big deal			
Say you're in a hurry			
Give simple directions			
Say someone or something is a bit...			
Say someone or something is so...			
Say someone or something is too...			
Say what bus or train you have to catch			
Ask or tell what time the next train leaves			
Ask or tell what platform it leaves from			
Buy the tickets			
Talk about travelling by plane in Europe			

Suggested procedure

STAGE 1

• *Preparatory activity*

To help your students come to grips with the 'shopping' vocabulary in this first section of the chapter, why not bring into class a shopping basket or trolley laden with the goods they will see in the **fotoromanzo**: a couple of onions, tomatoes and peppers (one red, one green) and some pumpkin; a steak or two and a chicken; a loaf of bread, a couple of rolls, some cheese and salami; a newspaper, a magazine and a couple of comics. Remember that the class has already met some of the key words and expressions: **fare la spesa, il pane, la verdura, il giornale, la rivista.**

You could introduce the topic by launching into a monologue: **Uffa, sono stanco/a! Ho fatto la spesa stamattina. Non mi piace fare la spesa. C'è un supermercato qui vicino. È aperto dalle otto fino alle nove di sera.**

Che cos'ho comprato oggi? Vediamo un po'. Ho comprato (*taking things from basket*) **della verdura; del pane, dei panini, del formaggio e del salame; due bistecche, un pollo; un giornale, una rivista e dei fumetti. E adesso non ho più soldi!!! Sono al verde** (*showing empty purse*).

Ti piace la verdura, Justin? Mangi la verdura a cena, Elena? Ah, qualche volta! Guardiamo la mia verdura! Ecco delle cipolle: una cipolla, due cipolle. Dei pomodori: un pomodoro, due pomodori. Dei peperoni: un peperone rosso, un peperone verde. E alla fine, un chilo di zucca. Ti piace la zucca, Richard?

You could then take time out to write these items on the board and to briefly explain your use of **del, della, dei, delle** to mean 'some'. Then ask the students to shop for the different items and put them back into your basket:

▲ **Desidera?**
■ **Vorrei dei pomodori.**
▲ **Ecco dei pomodori.**
■ **Grazie.**

It would also be interesting to show the class an Italian newspaper and a teen magazine as well as a couple of comics. You could introduce some of the leading comic characters such as **Topolino**, **Paperino**, **Braccio di Ferro** and **Dylan Dog**.

• *Maura fa la spesa* Textbook p 122

Before you read and listen to this **fotoromanzo** you could explain **aperto** and **chiuso**.

Note to the first printing of the Textbook: Whereas the photographic Sergio's Italian is flawless, his cartoon counterpart extended his butchery to the language. His blunder is obvious.

• *Penna in mano! A Maura fa la spesa I* Workbook p 116

• *In poche parole 1* Textbook p 125

The format of this exercise is unusual in that the dialogue is based on the photographs in the story **Maura fa la spesa**. Take the story one double-page spread at a time and look for the different shops. For the purpose of this exercise, **qui vicino** means somewhere on these two pages. Don't forget to include **il mercato** on page 123.

• *Penna in mano! C Che cosa compra Maura?* Workbook p 117

• *Su con l'orecchio! A Al mercato* Workbook p 114, Cassette 4, tape script Teacher's Manual p 71

• *A tu per tu 1* Textbook p 126

This exercise has an unusual format too, in that illustrations rather than words are used in one part of it. This, plus the fact that the same basic exchange is repeated for a number of items, gives it a decidedly **In poche parole**-esque feel.

The **gelato** and **frullato** illustrated here relate to the photo of the **gelateria** next to the exercise. Can your students think of any other examples of the **-eria** ending (**pizza–pizzeria, pane–panetteria**) to denote a shop?

• *Studiamo la lingua! A Preferisco i verbi* Workbook p 125

• *A lingua sciolta! 1 Fare la spesa* Textbook p 138

STAGE 2

• *Maura fa la spesa* Textbook p 122

Before you reread the story and listen to the tape again, draw attention to the expression **ho bisogno di...** Students who have mastered the expression **ho paura di** will have no trouble with this one!

• *Penna in mano! B Maura fa la spesa II* Workbook p 117

• *Penna in mano! D Chi compra che cosa dove?* Workbook p 118

For those having trouble distinguishing who's who, the identities of the characters depicted in this exercise are as follows:

1 Maura 2 Giorgio 3 Gigio 4 Dario 5 Francesco 6 Angelo 7 Antonio 8 Luisa 9 Scarno 10 Antonella

• *Rompicapi A I negozi* Workbook p 127

• *A tu per tu 2* Textbook p 126

The **aspirine** come from the **farmacia** in the picture alongside. It may be helpful to explain that **un generi alimentari** is an abbreviation of **un negozio di generi alimentari** (just as **il ferramenta** is often used instead of **il negozio di ferramenta**).

• *Su con l'orecchio! B Andiamo ai negozi!* Workbook p 114, Cassette 4, tape script Teacher's Manual p 72

• *Studiamo la lingua! D Del formaggio e della zucca* Workbook p 126

• *A tu per tu 3* Textbook p 127

Students will need to think whether they are going to the place (**al, alla, all'**) or the person who runs the place (**da**). You may have already mentioned the **-eria** ending as a common way of denoting 'a place that deals in...'. You could also point out the **-aio** ending as a common way of referring to 'a person who deals in...', hence **macelleria–macellaio**.

Does your class remember how to say 'I'm going to the dentist'? They went **dal medico** and **dal dentista** in **Capitolo 4**. Here they go **dal farmacista** and **alla farmacia**. You could mention that the **-ista** ending is another common ending to denote an occupation and that the article is **il** if the person is a man, **la** if it's a woman.

• *Studiamo la lingua! B Il mio verbo preferito* Workbook p 125

• *Su con l'orecchio! E Che cosa preferisci?* Workbook p 116, Cassette 4, tape script Teacher's Manual p 73

Use this listening exercise to prepare your class for the oral activity to follow.

• *A lingua sciolta! 2 Che cosa preferisci?* Textbook p 138, repromaster Teacher's Manual p 75

Two items which occur later in the chapter but are needed for this activity are **il cavolo** and **il maiale**.

STAGE 3

• *Franca cerca la neve* Textbook p 128

This **fotoromanzo** takes students out of the urban environment of Rome into the countryside of Tuscany. There is also a glimpse of **Siena** and Florence and of some smaller hillside towns.

The main new language topic is 'weather', but this is not followed up until after the **fumetto** entitled **Franca torna a Roma**. For the time being, your class can concentrate on comprehension of the **fotoromanzo**, enjoying its cultural content while they learn the new words and expressions they will need for future exercises and activities.

Franca was discovered road-skiing near the border between **Lazio** and **Toscana**. Your class could consult the map at the back of the book to pinpoint her location. **San Gimignano** (frame 2) and **Pittigliano** (frame 3) are included as examples of the hillside towns that are a big part of the attraction of this region.

Siena is the **città preferita** of many people, not just Franca. You might decide to dwell a little longer in this city and find some extra material to show your class, including, perhaps, some information and pictures on **il Palio**.

Surprisingly, given the Italians' penchant for **la caccia**, there are still some **cinghiali** left to roam the woods of Tuscany. The dulcet tones of the church bells share the morning stillness with the sharp reports of the hunter's **doppietta**.

You might like to point out just how **pericoloso** it would be to try skiing along an Italian **autostrada**, with drivers pushing their Alfa Romeos and (**magari**) their Ferraris to breathtaking speeds! This particular one is **l'Autostrada del Sole**, which allows you to rocket from **Milano** to **Napoli** in just a few hours. **Firenze**, by the way, will be featured more fully at a later stage of the *Forza!* course.

- *Domande* Textbook p 131

- *Penna in mano! E Franca cerca la neve I* Workbook p 119

- *Franca cerca la neve* Textbook p 128
Read and listen to the **fotoromanzo** again, concentrating this time on the words and expressions relating to the weather and the countryside.

- *Penna in mano! F Franca cerca la neve II* Workbook p 120

- *Penna in mano! G In campagna* Workbook p 121

- *In poche parole 3* Textbook p 137
For this exercise we fast forward a little, skipping over the **fumetto**. Franca has evidently come to grief and the images we see here are the product of a dazed consciousness. Your students will know the words for most of the animals, but will probably need you to tell them **il maiale** and **la mucca**, both of which occur in the **fumetto**. The activities can all be described by expressions with **fare**; the two that occur in the **fumetto** are **fare windsurf** and **fare lo sci acquatico**. Other expressions from the preceding **fumetto** are **Che cavolo succede?** and **Che strano!**

- *Studiamo la lingua! C In quella bella cappella* Workbook p 126

- *Penna in mano! K Che cavolo succede?* Workbook p 124

- *Su con l'orecchio! C Nella vecchia fattoria* Workbook p 115, Cassette 4, tape script Teacher's Manual p 72

1 What does Massimo eat?

2 Why does the vet say, '**Gli asini non sono veramente stupidi**'?

3 a Why has the farmer called the vet to Maria?
  b What is wrong with her?

4 What is strange about this sheep?

5 Why does the vet say '**poveretto**' to the lamb?

6 What does the vet mean when he says of the horse, '**Meno male che non ha i denti da lupo**'?

STAGE 4

- *Franca torna a Roma* Textbook p 132
This story completes the basic weather picture with two new expressions: **c'è vento** and **piove**. It also adds to the livestock: **il maiale** and **la mucca**. It also finishes off the food shopping with **il cavolo**, **il prosciutto** and **il latte**.

- *Penna in mano! H Franca torna a Roma* Workbook p 122

- *Su con l'orecchio! D Che tempo fa?* Workbook p 115, Cassette 4, tape script Teacher's Manual p 73

Once you have corrected this listening exercise allow your class to listen again to Franca's weather reports, matching them with the appropriate illustrations. This will serve as useful preparation for the following **In poche parole** exercise.

- *In poche parole 2* Textbook p 136

- *Penna in mano! I Che tempo fa?* Workbook p 123

- *Penna in mano! J Com'è il tempo?* Workbook p 124

- *Franca torna a Roma* Textbook p 132
Reread this **fumetto** and listen to the tape again.

- *Rompicapi B Quale?* Workbook p 128

- **Rompicapi C Troviamo le parole!**
  Workbook p 128

Solution: 1 **generi alimentari**
2 **fruttivendolo** 3 **mercato** 4 **macelleria**
5 **edicola** 6 **supermercato** 7 **panetteria**
8 **gelateria** 9 **bistecca** 10 **carne** 11 **salame**
12 **pasta** 13 **pane** 14 **gelato** 15 **cipolla** 16 **pollo**
17 **latte** 18 **panino** 19 **frutta** 20 **zucca**
21 **aperto** 22 **chiuso** 23 **farmacista**
24 **macellaio** 25 Tom Cruise 26 **Lucio** 27 **Maura**
28 **lupo** 29 **pecora** 30 **agnello** 31 **asino**
32 **gatto** 33 **maiale** 34 **mucca**

- **Rompicapi D Cruciverba**
  Workbook p 129

Solution:

Suggested assessment tasks

Listening

- **Su con l'orecchio! A Al mercato**
  Workbook p 114, Cassette 4, tape script Teacher's Manual p 71

- **Su con l'orecchio! B Andiamo ai negozi!** *Workbook p 114, Cassette 4, tape script Teacher's Manual p 72*

- **Su con l'orecchio! E Che cosa preferisci?** *Workbook p 116, Cassette 4, tape script Teacher's Manual p 73*

Speaking

- **A tu per tu 1** *Textbook p 126*
- **A tu per tu 3** *Textbook p 127*

- **In poche parole 2A or B**
  Textbook p 136
- **A lingua sciolta! 2 Che cosa preferisci?** *Textbook p 138, repromaster Teacher's Manual p 75*

Reading

- **Penna in mano! A Maura fa la spesa I** *Workbook p 116*
  or
- **Penna in mano! B Maura fa la spesa II** *Workbook p 117*
- **Penna in mano! H Franca torna a Roma** *Workbook p 122*

Writing

Penna in mano! D Chi compra che cosa dove? *Workbook p 118*

Penna in mano! F Franca cerca la neve II *Workbook p 120*

Penna in mano! I Che tempo fa? *Workbook p 123*

Su con l'orecchio! Tape scripts

A Al mercato

Listen to these vendors at the market calling out the prices of the things they have for sale. Write the prices on the appropriate tags.

1 – Signori e signore! Guardate questa bella zucca, solo 1500 lire al chilo! 1500 lire il chilo di zucca!

2 – Tutta roba buona! Tutta roba buona! Guardate questi peperoni dalla Sicilia. Peperoni gialli, peperoni rossi, tutti solo 2800 lire al chilo! Occhio al prezzo, 2800 lire il chilo.

3 – Che bella roba qui, signori e signore. Pomodori verdi dal Lazio, 3200 al chilo. Pomodori, 3200 lire.

4 – Polli freschi! 4900 lire al chilo! Polli freschi! 4900 lire al chilo! Prendete un bel pollo per la cena di stasera!

5 – Cipolle, comprate le vostre cipolle qui. Solo 1300 il chilo. Un chilo di cipolle per solo 1300 lire!

6 – Che cavolo volete? I miei cavoli sono buonissimi e costano solo 1500 al chilo. Cavoli, 1500 lire al chilo!

7 – Che bella roba! Che bella roba! Qui c'è il salame di cinghiale dalla Toscana, a solo 2900 lire il chilo. Una specialità toscana per solo 2900 lire al chilo.

8 – Comprate i vostri formaggi qui. Ho pecorino, ho parmigiano...e oggi ho del formaggio svizzero per solo 4700 lire il chilo. Un chilo di formaggio svizzero per solo 4700 lire.

B Andiamo ai negozi!

Listen for what these people have to get and work out where they are going. Write a number on the appropriate building below.

1 – Ciao!
 – Ah, ciao! Mi dispiace, non posso parlare adesso. Devo comprare della carne.
 – Della carne?
 – Sì, compro delle bistecche per la cena.
 – Ma tu sei vegetariana.
 – Sì. Le bistecche sono per i miei genitori.

2 – Fai la spesa?
 – Sì, e adesso devo comprare dei panini, del formaggio e del salame.
 – C'è un negozio qui vicino. Ah, eccolo!
 – Grazie. Arrivederci.
 – Ciao!

3 – Uffa! Scusa, mi dispiace.
 – Ah, sei tu!
 – Sì, sono io. Ma scusa, ho fretta. Devo comprare una rivista, un giornale e dei fumetti.
 – Va bene, scappa!

4 – Uffa, che caldo!
 – Ma cosa vuoi? È estate!
 – Io vado a comprare un frullato.
 – Un momento, vengo anch'io. Io voglio comprare un gelato.

5 – Vado a fare la spesa. Vuoi venire?
 – Sì, ma prima devo ritirare dei soldi.
 – Bene, anch'io ho bisogno di soldi.
 – Andiamo, allora.

6 – Uffa, finalmente! La spesa è finita!
 – Sì, meno male. Dove andiamo? A casa?
 – No, mettiamo questa roba nella macchina e andiamo a prendere un caffè!
 – Possiamo prendere anche una pasta?
 – Sì, come no!

C Nella vecchia fattoria

The vet has been called to an old farm in **Toscana** to check on the health of the animals. Write the appropriate number under each animal to show the order in which the vet sees them.

1 – Ciao, bello! Come si chiama?
 – Si chiama Massimo.
 – Massimo! Un bel nome per un maiale. E che cosa mangia?
 – Un po' di tutto. Ha un buon appetito!
 – Mmm, secondo me questo maiale sta benissimo!
 – Meno male.

2 – Arturo, vieni qui! Presto! Arturo! Mi dispiace, dottore, Arturo è molto ostinato!
 – È un asino tipico! Fa niente, io vado da lui. Mmm, Arturo fa molto lavoro?
 – Qualche volta. Se non vuole lavorare, non lavora.
 – Che fortunato! Gli asini non sono veramente stupidi! Arturo sta molto bene.

3 – Questa è Maria, dottore. Secondo me, non sta bene.
 – Perchè no?
 – È il latte, dottore. Non dà molto latte.
 – Quanti anni ha?
 – Dieci.
 – Maria non è ammalata, è vecchia. È stanca. Devi comprare una mucca nuova.
 – Va bene.

4 – Questa pecora è sana e allegra. Che cosa mangia?
 – Mangia formaggio, dottore. Preferisce il formaggio svizzero.
 – Che strano, una pecora che mangia il formaggio!

5 – Che carino! Come si chiama?
 – Non ha un nome. Lo chiamiamo 'l'agnello'.

– Poveretto, non hai un nome!

– Come sta l'agnello, dottore?

– È in perfetta salute!

– Meno male!

6 – Aiii! Il mio braccio! Che cavolo...?!

– Mi dispiace, il cavallo ha fame. Ha sempre una fame da lupo.

– Meno male che non ha i denti da lupo. Come sta questo cavallo?

– Sta benissimo, dottore. È forte, è veloce...

– Complimenti, signore. Questa fattoria è in perfetto ordine!

– Grazie, dottore. Arrivederci.

D Che tempo fa?

Where is Franca? Listen to her comments on the weather and write a number under the appropriate picture.

1 – Accidenti, il tempo è orribile qui! Non piove, non nevica, ci sono solo quelle nuvole grigie e nere. C'è anche un vento molto forte. Mamma mia, è troppo forte...Che cavolo... non posso sciare! Oooh! Volare, oo oo!

2 – Fa molto caldo oggi – 25 gradi! C'è un sole brillante, il cielo è azzurro...ma c'è solo un po' di neve. Devo sciare oggi. Secondo me la neve sarà finita domani.

3 – Fa bel tempo ma non sono contenta. È pericoloso sciare sulla strada. Ho bisogno di neve! Con questo cielo azzurro e questo sole molto forte, come può nevicare?

4 – Che cavolo...?! Adesso piove! Brrr, fa freddo. Ho bisogno di un cappuccino caldo. Che tempo orribile!

5 – Ah, che bel tempo! Fa freddo, ma c'è sole, il cielo è azzurro e c'è neve. Sì, c'è neve. Neve sulle montagne, neve sulle colline, neve sui campi, neve sugli alberi...Ciao pupazzo! Come stai?

6 – Che brutto tempo! È orribile! Che freddo! Non posso sciare con questo tempo. Non mi piace essere gelato così. Io vado a casa!

E Che cosa preferisci?

How well does Tony know Gemma? Listen to all of his predictions first and then see how well they match her answers. Since he is only doing half the survey give him two points for every correct answer.

Prima parte

1 – Mmm, l'aerobica o il jogging? Secondo me, Gemma preferisce l'aerobica.

2 – Il cappuccino o la Coca-Cola? Boh, non lo so. Segno il cappuccino.

3 – La carne o la verdura? Questo è facile, è vegetariana.

4 – Il cinema o la televisione? Mmm, secondo me preferisce il cinema. Va sempre al cinema con gli amici.

5 – La città o la campagna? Be', abita in città. Segno 'città'.

6 – Il formaggio o il salame? Facile – è vegetariana.

7 – Che cosa preferisce, i gelati o i frullati? Secondo me preferisce i gelati.

8 – I giallorossi o i biancocelesti? Secondo me, i biancocelesti.

9 – Preferisce l'inverno o l'estate? Ma tutti preferiscono l'estate, vero? Sì, l'estate.

10 – L'italiano o l'inglese? Facile! Tutti noi in questa classe preferiamo l'italiano!

Seconda parte

1 – Senti, Gemma, che cosa preferisci, l'aerobica o il jogging?

– L'aerobica! Odio il jogging!

2 – Va bene, che cosa preferisci, il cappuccino o la Coca-Cola?

– Non bevo il caffè, allora, la Coca-Cola.

3 – Gemma, che cosa preferisci, la carne o la verdura?

– Che domanda! Io sono vegetariana!

– Sì, lo so.

4 – Che cosa preferisci, il cinema o la televisione?

– Il cinema. I film alla televisione sono tutti vecchi.

5 – La città o la campagna, Gemma, che cosa preferisci?

   – Preferisco la campagna.

   – La campagna?! Perchè?

   – Be', non so. I campi, le pecore, le mucche, gli alberi...

   – Va bene, va bene...

6 – Preferisci il formaggio al salame, vero?

   – Sì.

7 – Che cosa preferisci, Gemma, i gelati o i frullati?

   – Non mangio mai i frullati.

   – Segno i gelati?

   – I gelati, sì. Amo i gelati.

   – Anch'io. Vuoi venire alla gelateria dopo la scuola?

   – Mmm, non so.

8 – Che cosa preferisci, i giallorossi o i biancocelesti?

   – Non so, che cosa sono?

   – Sono squadre di calcio.

   – Io preferisco la squadra romana.

   – Sono tutte e due squadre romane.

   – Va bene, i biancocelesti!

   – Brava!

9 – Preferisci l'inverno o l'estate, Gemma?

   – Preferisco l'inverno.

   – Non ci credo! Perchè?

   – Perchè mi piace sciare. Non posso sciare d'estate!

10 – L'italiano o l'inglese, Gemma?

   – Ma tu lo sai. In questa classe preferiamo l'italiano, vero?

Che cosa preferisci?

Nome _____ Classe _____

Amico/a _____

Che cosa preferisci?

secondo me _secondo te_		_secondo me_ _secondo te_	
❏ ❏ aerobica	❏ ❏ jogging
❏ ❏ cappuccino	❏ ❏ Coca-Cola
❏ ❏ carne	❏ ❏ verdura
❏ ❏ cinema	❏ ❏ televisione
❏ ❏ città	❏ ❏ campagna
❏ ❏ formaggio	❏ ❏ salame
❏ ❏ gelati	❏ ❏ frullati
❏ ❏ i giallorossi	❏ ❏ i biancocelesti
❏ ❏ inverno	❏ ❏ estate
❏ ❏ italiano	❏ ❏ inglese
❏ ❏ lasagne	❏ ❏ spaghetti
❏ ❏ maiale	❏ ❏ agnello
❏ ❏ mercato	❏ ❏ supermercato
❏ ❏ pollo	❏ ❏ bistecca
❏ ❏ riviste	❏ ❏ fumetti
❏ ❏ Roma	❏ ❏ Siena
❏ ❏ sport	❏ ❏ musica
❏ ❏ treno	❏ ❏ autobus
❏ ❏ violino	❏ ❏ chitarra
❏ ❏ zucca	❏ ❏ cavolo

20 punti – Are you sure you're not twins?!

15–19 punti – You are _very_ good friends.

10–15 punti – You can still surprise each other, can't you?

5–10 punti – You don't really know each other that well, do you?

0–5 punti – Are you sure you've been introduced?

In the **io** column, give yourself a tick for each thing that you know how to do in Italian. Then ask a friend to check you and mark the **amico/a** column. Keep the last column free for when your teacher has time to hear how you are progressing.

Nome _____ Classe _____

Capitolo 7	io	amico/a	
Tell someone not to forget something			
Ask if there is a certain shop nearby			
Say 'There it is!'			
Say that it's closed			
Say that it's open			
Ask people what they prefer			
Say what you prefer			
Say what you need			
Say what you would like			
Shop at the butcher's			
Shop at the greengrocer's			
Shop at the newsagent's			
Shop at the market			
Ask what the weather is like			
Say that it's fine			
Say that it's awful			
Describe a warm, sunny day			
Describe a cold, cloudy day			
Describe a windy, rainy or snowy day			
Say that you're starving			
Talk about (and to) some farm animals			
Ask what the hell is happening			

Suggested procedure

STAGE 1

- *Preparatory activity*

You could set the scene for this final chapter by bringing into class a big bag or two containing those small, snack-size packets of different types of **croccantini**. With everyone in possession – and possession is linguistically important in this chapter – of their own little parcel of realia, motivation will be high as you introduce the new theme:

Ho una fame da lupo. Quando è l'ora del pranzo? All'una!! Mamma mia, non posso aspettare. Devo trovare qualcosa da mangiare. Ah, ecco un sacco interessante. Vediamo un po'...

Mmm, questi croccantini sono buoni. Gnam! Ah, anche tu vuoi mangiare dei croccantini, Karen? Ecco un sacchetto per te...un sacchetto per te...I miei sono croccantini al formaggio. I tuoi? Ah, i tuoi sono patatine. Posso provare i tuoi? Vuoi provare i miei? Ti piace il gusto del formaggio?

Basta, basta! Anche Kelly ha dei croccantini al formaggio. Perchè non mangi i suoi?

Ehi, ragazzi, buttate le carte lì!

Why not write some of the key new words and expressions on the board before opening the *Textbook* and switching on the cassette recorder?

- *Un uomo moderno* Textbook p 141

The introduction of fast food into Italy is still a sore point with many people and the gastronomic tug-of-war taking place in the Ferraro family is an oft-repeated one throughout the country.

The opening of the first McDonald's in **Piazza di Spagna** (see the map on page 185) in 1986 caused a furore, even though the company made an attempt to make the architecture and, to a certain extent, the cuisine blend as much as possible with the local environment. There are a few shots of this restaurant in the story entitled **Da McDonald's** on page 146. There are now half-a-dozen or so McDonald's in the Eternal City.

You could ask your students for their reaction to Antonio's remonstration: **Non capisco! Siete italiani ma preferite mangiare quella roba americana!**

If Italy has imported the Big Mac, it has also exported the pizza. Your students should be able to join in a discussion about this famous food: **Mangi la pizza, Melanie? Ti piace? Qual è la tua pizza preferita? Ah, la pizza Hawaiiana! Che cosa c'è sulla Hawaiiana? Ananas! Ananas su una pizza! Non ci credo!**

Vai ad una pizzeria o mangi la pizza a casa? C'è una buona pizzeria qui vicino? (If the answer is in the affirmative, someone may suggest a class visit!)

- *Penna in mano! A Un uomo moderno I* Workbook p 134

There may be some room for debate in deciding which explanation is the best. In question 3, for example, although answer b is intended as the correct one, you may find vigorous proponents of answer a or c. If that is the case, keep in mind that comprehension is the key here, so that if a student's divergent choice is based on a correct understanding of the language, but a different interpretation of character or situation, there is no need to insist on marking that answer 'wrong'.

- *Studiamo la lingua! A È il mio o il tuo?* Workbook p 144

- *Su con l'orecchio! A Lo snack perfetto* Workbook p 130, Cassette 4, tape script Teacher's Manual p 81

Before switching on the recorder it would be a good idea to have the class look closely at the various packets displayed in the *Workbook*. Each one has a key phrase or two which will provide them with the clues they need to understand which snack is being advertised. You might ask your students to tell you which expressions refer to the taste, which to the price, which to the quantity and which to any prizes or special offers. You might decide to read through the tape scripts and pick out some words or phrases for some special treatment.

- *Penna in mano! C La Maddalena*
Workbook p 136

- *In poche parole 1A Textbook p 145*
To set the scene for this and the following exercise, you could ask your students to imagine that these mini-dialogues are taking place in a restaurant between a customer and a waiter, or between a customer new to Italian food and a companion who is in-the-know.

Before they attempt this exercise, students will need to practise pronouncing the different ingredients mentioned on this page.

- *In poche parole 1B Textbook p 145*

STAGE 2

- *Un uomo moderno Textbook p 141*
Reread the story and listen to the tape again. You may find your class ready, willing and able to role-play the story at this stage.

- *Domande Textbook p 144*

- *Penna in mano! B Un uomo moderno II Workbook p 135*

- *Studiamo la lingua! B È il suo! Workbook p 144*

- *In poche parole 1C Textbook p 145*

- *In poche parole 1D Textbook p 145*
Alert the class to the need to change **piace** to **piacciono** in certain cases. Can they tell you which ones?

- *Studiamo la lingua! C Adadiinsu?! Workbook p 145*

- *Studiamo la lingua! D Su! Forza! Workbook p 145*

- *Su con l'orecchio! B La Maddalena Workbook p 131, Cassette 4, tape script Teacher's Manual p 82*
There is quite a bit of detail for students to listen for, so don't hesitate to pause the tape between 'tables'. Once they have completed the exercise, give your students the opportunity to listen again for some of the finer detail of the conversations between waiter and diners.

STAGE 3

- *Da McDonald's Textbook p 146*
Your students will probably be struck by the muted tones of the building and the almost apologetic dimensions of the Golden Arches **alla romana**. Anyone doubting the popularity of the **motorino** as a means of transport for young people need look no further!

The **insalata mista** mentioned in frame 7 is available from a separate salad bar in an Italian McDonald's. Your class will also notice that **birra** is readily available, along with the mineral water and fruit juice. A recent survey in Italy revealed that nearly two-thirds of Italian young people regarded beer as a non-alcoholic beverage – this in spite of the fact that the local product is similar in strength to beers around the world.

The statue in frame 9 is part of an attempt to give the interior of McDonald's in **Piazza di Spagna** a flavour of classical antiquity. Frame 11 shows a couple of the Roman vistas that abound in the trompe l'oeil decorations around the walls of the restaurant.

(Note that there is a spelling error in Frame 18 on page 149 of the *Textbook*. The coffee cannister should of course be labelled **caffè**. You could ask your students to see if they can spot the error.)

- *Penna in mano! D Da McDonald's Workbook p 137*
You may find this story more manageable if you treat the lunch-time escapade and the following morning's breakfast separately. In that case you would do the first nine questions before moving on to **La mattina dopo**.

- *A tu per tu 2 Textbook p 152*

- *Su con l'orecchio! C Da McDonald's Workbook p 132, Cassette 4, tape script Teacher's Manual p 82*

- *A tu per tu 1 Textbook p 152*
Students will find it easier to choose if they have the 'cards' from the previous listening exercise open in front of them, along with the board in frame 6, page 147 of the *Textbook*.

- *In poche parole 1E Textbook p 145*
We rewind to this exercise to revise asking and

giving prices, in preparation for the **Quanto costa?** exercises to follow.

- *Penna in mano! E Quanto costa?* *Workbook p 138*

Someone in the class may realise that the L. 1700 price quoted for **cappuccino e cornetto** is a special for the months of November and December. Someone else may be interested to know that **Via Tiburtina** is off the map of Rome to the east, straight out to the right from **Stazione Termini**. What do we call **cornetti** in English?

- *Quanto costa? Textbook p 153*

- *Penna in mano! F Buon appetito!* *Workbook p 139*

- *In poche parole 2A Textbook p 151*

You could prepare your class for this and the following exercise by introducing two simpler dialogues:

▲ Che cosa prendi da mangiare?
■ Io prendo le lasagne.
▲ Che cosa vorresti da bere?
■ Io vorrei un'acqua minerale.

- *In poche parole 2B Textbook p 151*

- *Penna in mano! G Mangiamo all'italiana! Workbook p 140*

- *La mensa Textbook p 153*

- *In poche parole 2C Textbook p 151*

STAGE 4

- *Buon Natale in Piazza Navona* *Textbook p 154*

Pierluigi is busking outside one of the restaurants that line sections of **Piazza Navona**. He is not the only one to nominate this one as his favourite Roman square! Your students will be able to find it on the map on page 185 of the *Textbook*.

It is not wise to launch into a series of generalisations about Christmas in Italy, since practices vary from region to region and family to family. Some families have yielded to (probably) American influence and welcome **Babbo Natale**

down their chimneys. Others put off present-giving until the eve of January 6, the **Epifania** (or **Befana**), the day set aside to commemorate the Magi's gifts to the baby Jesus. On this evening, the **Befana** makes her gift-laden way down the chimneys of houses where good children live. She spends the rest of the year scaring hell out of naughty ones. Some Italians will tell you that nobody uses Christmas stockings in Italy, but someone must be buying the ones we see displayed here in **Piazza Navona**.

The foods displayed in frame 13 are all manifestations of **marzapane**. Some of the **burattini** in frame 14, including **Braccio di Ferro** and **i Puffi** (one wearing a **cappuccio rosso**), will already be familiar to your students. Some will pick up on the prominent proboscis of **Pinocchio**. The Disney ducks are destined for some closer attention on page 157. Laurel and Hardy are called **Stanlio e Ollio** in Italy. Some of the others are characters from the popular puppet show **Pulcinella**. One character who does not get a guernsey is **Cappuccetto Rosso** (Red Riding Hood).

- *Penna in mano! H Buon Natale in Piazza Navona! I Workbook p 140*

- *Domande Textbook p 157*

- *Penna in mano! I Buon Natale in Piazza Navona! II Workbook p 141*

- *Su con l'orecchio! D Buon Natale! Workbook p 133, Cassette 4, tape script Teacher's Manual p 83*

- *Una ricetta per spaghetti alla bolognese Textbook p 158*

This recipe is offered as a basis for some practical work in the kitchen, perhaps resulting in a **pranzo di Natale** for your class. Students could work together in small groups, using the vocabulary to help them read the recipe and then produce the goods.

The vocabulary on this page is obviously passive, i.e. intended for comprehension for this specific purpose only. The **rompicapi** in this chapter do include a few words from this list, but it is assumed that students will hunt unto the nether regions of all chapters to solve the more difficult puzzle clues.

• *Rompicapi A Una fame da lupo*
Workbook p 146

Solution: 1 **pollo** 2 **olio** 3 **pizzeria**
4 **all'italiana** 5 **pomodoro** 6 **pancetta** 7 **Flash**
8 **Napoli** 9 **formaggio** 10 **insalata mista**
11 **cucina** 12 **Fonzies** 13 McDonald's

• *A lingua sciolta! Che cosa vorresti?*
Textbook p 159, repromaster Teacher's Manual p 84

• *Rompicapi B Troviamo le parole!*
Workbook p 147

Solution: 1 **caramello** 2 **cioccolato** 3 **vaniglia**
4 **fragola** 5 **acqua gassata** 6 **birra** 7 **succo d'arancia** 8 **tè** 9 **caffè** 10 **cena** 11 **colazione**
12 **pranzo** 13 **formaggio** 14 **manzo** 15 **sale**
16 **basilico** 17 **pepe** 18 **piccione** 19 **fontana**
20 **mercato di natale** 21 **sacco** 22 **calza**
23 **regalo**

Pierluigi's final message: **Buon Natale!**

• *Penna in mano! J Buon Natale in Piazza Navona! III Workbook p 142*

Most will find this activity quite challenging, both to their imagination and their language skills. It will probably be productive to have a preparatory discussion in class, calling for suggestions from the floor. Encourage them to go beyond **ciao!** and **come stai?**

If they are really struggling for ideas you could make suggestions along the following lines:

1 The artist could be thinking, 'Great! There are lots of people here today so I'll be able to get lots of money.' (Frame 2, *Textbook*)

2 One **carabiniere** could be saying, 'Look at that idiot. That hair is ridiculous.' The other could reply, 'I like his hair. I'd like to have hair like that.' (Frame 4, *Textbook*)

3 The statue could complain, 'I've got a hard job. There are always lots of pigeons here.' (Frame 5, *Textbook*)

4 **La Befana** would probably be saying, 'Be good, children, if you want a heap of presents.' (Frame 7, *Textbook*)

5 This one is probably saying, 'Goodness me! This chimney is too small!' (Frame 9, *Textbook*)

6 'I'm small but I'm very good at soccer.' (Frame 2, *Textbook*)

7 The stallholder could be saying, 'These bread rolls and this fruit are not real: it's all marzipan.' (Frame 13, *Textbook*)

8 Popeye's line is obvious: 'I'm so strong because I eat up all my spinach.' (Frame 14, *Textbook*)

• *Che cosa c'è nelle calze dei ragazzi?*
Textbook p 161

• *Penna in mano! K Nelle calze dei ragazzi Workbook p 143*

It might be fun to discuss with your class what **la Befana** is saying here. Press them until they have come up with a whole range of imaginative possibilities. You could even offer **un regalo speciale** to whoever comes up with the best suggestion.

• *Penna in mano! L Una lettera a Babbo Natale o alla Befana Workbook p 143, repromaster Teacher's Manual p 85*

• *Rompicapi C Cruciverba*
Workbook p 148

Solution:

Crossword solution answers: 5 NATALE, 6 POMODORO, 7 FRAGOLE, 9 CARO, 10 ETTI, 11 CROCCANTINI, 12 CUCINARE, 15 CARAMELLE, 16 GEMELLI, 20 CARABINIERI, 21 CALZA, 22 CAMINO, 25 ARANCIA, 26 CASSERUOLA, 27 GENTE

Suggested assessment tasks

Listening

• *Su con l'orecchio! B La Maddalena Workbook p 131, Cassette 4, tape script Teacher's Manual p 82*

• *Su con l'orecchio! C Da McDonald's*

Workbook p 132, Cassette 4, tape script
Teacher's Manual p 82

- *Su con l'orecchio! D Buon Natale!*
  Workbook p 133, Cassette 4, tape script
  Teacher's Manual p 83

Speaking

- *In poche parole 2A and B*
  Textbook p 151

- *A tu per tu 1* *Textbook p 152*

- *A tu per tu 2* *Textbook p 152*

- *A lingua sciolta! Che cosa vorresti?*
  Textbook p 159, repromaster Teacher's
  Manual p 84

Reading

- *Penna in mano! A Un uomo moderno I*
  Workbook p 134

or

- *Penna in mano! B Un uomo moderno*
  II Workbook p 135

- *Penna in mano! H Buon Natale in*
  Piazza Navona! I Workbook p 140

 or

- *Penna in mano! I Buon Natale in*
  Piazza Navona! II Workbook p 141

Writing

- *Penna in mano! F Buon appetito!*
  Workbook p 139

- *Penna in mano! J Buon Natale in*
  Piazza Navona! III Workbook p 142

- *Penna in mano! L Una lettera a*
  Babbo Natale o alla Befana Workbook
  p 143, repromaster Teacher's Manual p 85

Su con l'orecchio!
Tape scripts

A Lo snack perfetto

Listen to these radio commercials for different foods. Write a number next to the appropriate packet or container to show which one is being advertised.

1 – Mmm, il gusto del formaggio! Crunch, munch. È sono così croccanti! Se volete uno snack delizioso, cercate il famoso sacchetto giallo e rosso. Questi sono gli originali! E adesso ci sono 100 grammi di gusto! Presto, andate al supermercato e comprate questi croccantini deliziosissimi...e buon appetito!

2 – È l'una e mezza, la scuola è finita, è quasi l'ora del pranzo...ma tu non puoi aspettare! Ecco lo snack perfetto per te! Apri il sacchetto e prova il gusto stuzzicante del formaggio! Questi sono i croccantini per i ragazzi moderni! Crunch, munch. Mmm, gustosissimi! E adesso c'è un regalo speciale per te. Mangia solo 18 sacchetti e puoi vincere una delle 30 000 T-shirt!

3 – Ecco il nuovo snack da Ferrero! Leggero, croccante, con il gusto delizioso del cioccolato. Quando hai una fame da lupo, quando hai bisogno di energia, prova qualcosa di dolce, qualcosa di buono. E non devi spendere tutti i tuoi soldi: costano solo 1600 lire per cinque pezzi. Sì, in ogni pacchetto ci sono cinque pezzi per solo 1600 lire. E se compri un pacchetto puoi cancellare e vincere uno di 30 000 karaoke. Che cosa aspetti?

4 – Sei stufo della solita colazione, vero? Il solito panino, la solita marmellata...Che noia! Ecco un'idea nuova: il gusto fresco e croccante del riso italiano! E questa non è solo una colazione da mangiare, è una colazione da ascoltare...Aggiungi un po' di latte...aspetta un momento...Ecco! Lo senti? Che miracolo! Compra un pacchetto e fai una colazione deliziosa e divertente!

5 – Finalmente, uno snack che fa bene alla salute! Questo è lo snack che mangiano in Francia, in America, in Australia – in quaranta paesi del mondo. Prova il gusto naturale di frutta! Gnam, gnam! Aah, gli aromi naturali dei frutti di bosco! Per il tuo appetito e per la tua salute, puoi mangiarlo a colazione, a pranzo, a cena, o come lo snack perfetto per ogni giorno.

6 – Quando fai la spesa, non dimenticare uno snack per i ragazzi. Compra le patatine perfette – gustosissime, deliziosissime, croccantissime! E adesso c'è un'offerta speciale – i Verdi Amici. Che cosa sono? Sono pupazzetti simpatici dai capelli verdi...e c'è un pupazzetto in ogni sachetto.

B La Maddalena

Take down the orders for each of these tables at **La Maddalena pizzeria** and **spaghetteria**. In some cases you can just tick the item ordered, but in others you may have to cross something out or add something in.

Tavolo 1

- Siete pronti per ordinare?
- Sì. Io prendo una pizza margherita e un'insalata mista.
- Una margherita e un'insalata. Va bene.
- Per me, spaghetti alla bolognese.
- Uno spaghetti bologna.
- Io vorrei una pizza boscaiola. Posso avere una boscaiola senza carciofi?
- Sì, come no!
- Grazie. Non mi piacciono i carciofi.
- Bene, una boscaiola senza carciofi...e poi?
- Io prendo gli spaghetti ai quattro formaggi.
- Benissimo. Grazie.

Tavolo 2

- Possiamo ordinare adesso?
- Sì, certo. Avanti.
- Allora, io vorrei spaghetti alla carbonara.
- Una carbonara.
- Io prendo una pizza. Avete la pizza al salmone oggi?
- Sì, c'è. Con un po' d'insalata?
- Ottima idea! Prendo anche un'insalata mista.
- Voglio ordinare una pizza con prosciutto, funghi e olive, ma non c'è.
- Perchè non facciamo una capricciosa e mettiamo anche dei funghi?
- Si può?
- Come no! Va bene, una capricciosa coi funghi. È tutto?
- Sì, grazie.

Tavolo 3

- Scusi, vorrei una caprese e un'insalata mista.
- Sì, signora.
- Ma sulla caprese vorrei anche del prosciutto, si può?
- Si può.
- E vorrei l'insalata senza pomodoro. Non posso mangiare il pomodoro.
- Va bene.

- E senza cipolla. Sono allergico alla cipolla.
- Va bene.
- E il mio amico prende una vegetariana con prosciutto.
- Ma no, non si può fare una vegetariana con prosciutto.
- Non si può? Non ci credo! Il mio amico vuole una vegetariana con prosciutto!
- Va bene, una vegetariana con prosciutto. Uffa!

Tavolo 4

- Io prendo una pizza napoli, ma vorrei anche del prosciutto.
- Allora, perchè non facciamo una capricciosa?
- Va bene. Possiamo mettere anche dei carciofi e dei peperoni?
- Sì, tutto è possibile. Ma perchè non facciamo una maddalena?
- Che cosa c'è su una maddalena?
- Un po' di tutto.
- Benissimo. Prendo una maddalena.
- Una maddalena. Ottima idea!

C Da McDonald's

It is a very busy lunch time at McDonald's in **Piazza di Spagna**. Mark each cusomer's order on the cards below.

1 – Buongiorno.
- Buongiorno. Allora, un Big Mac e una porzione media di patatine fritte.
- Va bene. Qualcosa da bere?
- Una Coca-Cola.
- Grande, media...?
- Grande.
- Qualcosa dalla pasticceria?
- No, come dessert prendo un sundae.
- Un sundae come?
- Al cioccolato.
- È tutto?
- Sì, grazie.

2 – Una patatine grande e una torta di mele, per favore.
- Una patatine grande e una torta di mele. Qualcosa da bere?
- No, grazie.

– Ah, mi dispiace, le patatine fritte sono finite. Deve aspettare un momento.

– Va bene, aspetto. E prendo anche un'insalata mista.

– E un'insalata. L'insalata è lì in fondo. Un momento, le patatine sono quasi pronte.

3 – Buongiorno. Desidera?

– Vorrei un panino di pollo e un succo d'arancia.

– Un panino di pollo e un succo d'arancia. Un dessert?

– Mmm, sì, perchè no! Un cono gelato, per favore.

– È tutto?

– Sì, basta così, grazie.

4 – Come si chiamano quei piccoli pezzi di pollo?

– Sono Chicken McNuggets.

– Va bene, prendo sei Chicken McNuggets e delle patatine fritte...una porzione piccola.

– Un dessert, qualcosa da bere?

– Sì, vorrei un tè freddo, per favore.

5 – Buongiorno. Desidera?

– Sì, che cosa c'è in un Cheeseburger?

– Carne, formaggio e una salsa di pomodoro.

– Che tipo di carne?

– È manzo, puro manzo.

– Va bene, un Cheeseburger, e un'acqua gassata e un sundae.

– Come vuole il sundae: vaniglia, cioccolato...?

– Caramello.

– È tutto?

– È tutto, sì.

6 – Scusi, che cos'è il Filet-o-Fish?

– È pesce.

– Be', non mi piace il pesce. Prendo un Big Mac. E poi...mmm, vediamo...

– Delle patatine fritte?

– Sì, una porzione grande, per favore.

– Qualcosa da bere...un tè, un caffè...?

– No, fa troppo caldo per il caffè. Prendo un succo d'arancia.

– Un dessert?

– No, grazie.

D Buon Natale!

Maura is giving out the Christmas presents on Christmas Eve. Draw lines to connect the present with the person who receives it.

– Ah, che carini! Qui ho due burattini, uno per Francesco, l'altro per Lucio. Vediamo...sì, Braccio di Ferro per Francesco e un Puffo per Lucio.

– Grazie, mamma.

– Non son' da me, sono dalla Befana. E qui, una bella pentola nuova. È per me? No, è per Antonio. Ecco, tesoro, adesso puoi cucinare un bel pranzo di Natale.

– Grazie, tesoro. Molto gentile.

– Grazie alla Befana! Adesso due lecca-lecca. Chi tifa per la Roma?

– Io.

– Va bene, Francesco, questo è per te, e questo lecca-lecca bianco e azzurro e per te, Lucio. Fantastico, dei nuovi pattini! Per chi sono? Mamma mia, sono per me! Grazie, Befana, adesso posso pattinare nel parco!...Un pallone! Ecco, è per te, Francesco. E per Lucio, che cosa c'è? Una nuova chitarra! Che fortunato che sei, Lucio!...E sacchetti di caramelle! Vediamo, c'è ne uno per Lucio, uno per Francesco, uno per Antonio e uno per me! Siamo fortunati, vero? Auguri a tutti!

– Buon Natale!

Che cosa vorresti?

È il tempo di organizzare qualcosa di speciale per la fine dell'anno. Perchè non fate un picnic, un barbecue o una festa? Per preparare il menù, dovete sapere che cosa preferiscono i vostri amici.

Fate queste domande ai membri della vostra classe. Possono dare due o tre risposte se vogliono.

Nome _____ Classe _____

1 Che tipo di carne vorresti?
- [ ] a la bistecca
- [ ] b l'agnello
- [ ] c il manzo tritato (per hamburger)
- [ ] d il pollo

2 Che cosa vorresti nei panini?
- [ ] a il prosciutto
- [ ] b il formaggio
- [ ] c il salame
- [ ] d l'insalata

3 Che tipo di snack vorresti?
- [ ] a dei croccantini
- [ ] b delle caramelle
- [ ] c delle paste
- [ ] d dei lecche-lecche

4 Che gusto di gelato vorresti?
- [ ] a la vaniglia
- [ ] b la fragola
- [ ] c il caramello
- [ ] d il cioccolato

5 Da bere che cosa vorresti?
- [ ] a succo d'arancia
- [ ] b Coca-Cola
- [ ] c acqua minerale
- [ ] d tè

6 Che cosa vorresti mettere nell'insalata?
- [ ] a dei pomodori
- [ ] b delle cipolle
- [ ] c dei funghi
- [ ] d dei peperoni

7 Che tipo di frutta vorresti?
- [ ] a delle mele
- [ ] b delle fragole
- [ ] c delle arancie
- [ ] d delle banane

Una lettera alla Befana

Cara Befana,

Mi chiamo Travis Stevens, ho dodici anni e abito a **12 Moss Street, Mill Park**. Mi dispiace, ma quando vieni da me, non puoi scendere per il camino perchè è chiuso. Devi entrare per la porta. La chiave è sotto l'albero di Natale in giardino.

Io vorrei una nuova console Super Nintendo a 16 Bit. Vorrei anche il controller e il trasformatore. Posso anche avere un nuovo videogioco? Vorrei Donkey Kong Country o i Puffi. Tutti i miei amici giocano con i videogiochi.

Se non posso avere i videogiochi, vorrei un pallone e una chitarra elettrica. Non suono la chitarra ma voglio imparare. Se c'è posto nella mia calza, vorrei anche qualcosa da mangiare: un lecca-lecca e un sacchetto di Fonzies. (Sono goloso!)

Io faccio sempre il bravo. Aiuto mamma e papà, faccio il mio letto, faccio i piatti e gioco con il mio piccolo fratello. Mangio la verdura a cena (ma non il cavolo — odio il cavolo!). Sono un angelo!

Tu puoi lasciare i miei regali nella mia grande calza verde e rossa. Per te, lascio qualcosa da mangiare e da bere sulla tavola in cucina. Ti piace la birra e la pizza fredda?

Grazie, Befana, e Buon Natale!

Il tuo amico,

Travis Stevens

Forza! uno student progress sheet

In the **io** column, give yourself a tick for each thing that you know how to do in Italian. Then ask a friend to check you and mark the **amico/a** column. Keep the last column free for when your teacher has time to hear how you are progressing.

Nome _____ **Classe** _____

Capitolo 8	io	amico/a	
Say that it's lunch time			
Ask what we're having for lunch			
Say there's nothing to eat			
Suggest that you go out to eat			
Say that you (don't) want to eat Italian			
Say that's a great idea			
Tell someone 'That's enough!'			
Ask someone why they are taking your...			
Ask why they don't take his or her...			
Say that you don't understand			
Ask what's on a certain pizza			
Say what foods you can't eat			
Ask someone what they would like			
Say what you'll have			
Say something is yummy			
Ask someone why they're not finishing...			
Ask what we're having for breakfast			
Order a meal at McDonald's			
Say that something is expensive			
Name the Disney ducks			
Wish someone Merry Christmas			

Capitolo 8